Overcoming Barriers
to Evangelization
in Japan

Overcoming Barriers *to* Evangelization *in* Japan

DAVID J. LU

WIPF *&* STOCK · Eugene, Oregon

OVERCOMING BARRIERS TO EVANGELIZATION IN JAPAN

Copyright © 2019 David J. Lu. All rights reserved. Except for brief quotations in critical publications or reviews, no part of this book may be reproduced in any manner without prior written permission from the publisher. Write: Permissions, Wipf and Stock Publishers, 199 W. 8th Ave., Suite 3, Eugene, OR 97401.

Wipf & Stock
An Imprint of Wipf and Stock Publishers
199 W. 8th Ave., Suite 3
Eugene, OR 97401

www.wipfandstock.com

PAPERBACK ISBN: 978-1-5326-9274-1
HARDCOVER ISBN: 978-1-5326-9275-8
EBOOK ISBN: 978-1-5326-9276-5

Manufactured in the U.S.A.   04/18/19

Unless otherwise noted, all biblical citations are from the New King James Version. Copyright © 1982 by Thomas Nelson, Inc. Used by permission. All rights reserved.

Contents

Note | vii
Preface | ix

Chapter 1
Barrier I: Self | 1

Chapter 2
Barrier II: Buddhism Enmeshed in Japanese Culture | 9

Chapter 3
Barrier III: Myriad Deities of Shintoism | 37

Chapter 4
Barrier IV: Seeking Perfection Without God | 53

Chapter 5
Barrier V: Invisible Proscription | 73

Chapter 6
Solution I: Walking With Christ | 85

Chapter 7
Solution II: Learning from Business Practices | 93

Epilogue
Good and Faithful Church Planter | 114

Name Index | 121
Subject Index | 123
Scripture Index | 127

Note

Japanese names are given in this book in the Japanese order, that is, the surname precedes the given name. The Hepburn-Reischauer system of Romanization is used. No macron sign is used to distinguish long and short vowels.

Chinese names are also given in the traditional order, that is, the surname precedes the given name. The pinyin Romanization system, with a few exceptions, is utilized throughout this volume.

Preface

"Go, therefore, and make disciples of all the nations," were the last words of Jesus before he ascended to heaven. Why then do close to 99 percent of the Japanese people still not accept Christ? The proscription against Christianity was removed in 1873 and nearly one and one half centuries have since passed. Buddhism entered Japan in 552, and two centuries later the great Buddha in Nara was erected. By then Buddhism had become the official religion of the realm. Times and circumstances differ. Yet today as Christians we must seriously examine why Christianity has not been able to make significant inroads into Japanese society.

Buddhism blended into Japanese culture and became part of the fabric of Japan. As for Christianity, it remains an alien religion from the west. Jesus of Nazareth was a Jew and not a Westerner. Yet there has been very little effort made by the Christian community in Japan to contextualize its doctrine into Japanese culture.

I taught Japanese history to generations of students in which an understanding of Shinto and Buddhism was always a critical component. In this book, bear with me to learn the success story of Buddhism and observe why animistic Shinto still holds sway over modern Japan. Why couldn't Christianity be as appealing to the Japanese? It is a puzzle which is difficult to answer. As a cultural historian, I have been dazzled by Japan's accomplishments. It is, however, the weight of their glorious tradition that has created various barriers to the acceptance of Christ. Travel with me to find

Preface

the glory of Japanese civilization, and discover how we may overcome these barriers it has created.

This book, however, is not a historical treatise. It is a note by an old retired professor who, before receiving his PhD, was a theological student. It is a foray into my first and most abiding love, with a passion to share my findings with you who are missionaries to Japan.

It may sound presumptuous on my part to present my findings to you who have been in the forefront of battle against unbelief. But forgive me in saying this. I have had the advantage of being able to observe Japanese society from within (*uchi*), which as *gaijin* (*soto*) you cannot.

Born in Taiwan in 1928 when it was under Japanese rule, I was a Japanese citizen through my high school years, receiving their best education. In my academic career as a Japan specialist, I developed close contact with all strata of Japanese society. It was by luck that I got to know seventeen prime ministers personally. The Nobel Laureate Sato Eisaku became a close personal friend. I visited 120 businesses and factories, but did not neglect to observe the homeless. Aside from visiting a house church for the homeless in Asakusa, I spent many early summer morning hours in Tokyo's Ueno Park witnessing how the homeless managed their lives.

Weaving my experiences together, I am trying to present a picture of how missionary messages might be perceived by those who are on the receiving end. I have also prepared a Japanese version of this book and those Japanese friends who have read it agree that this book's information comes from within (*uchi*) and represents their views well. It is this information I want to share with you. You will find that this is not a traditional missionary handbook. It is unconventional and includes techniques borrowed from business practices to solve mission problems. I hope this little volume will be of help to you in leading your friends to Christ in Japan.

Chapter 1

Barrier I
Self

As CHRISTIANS, WE HAVE an obligation to share with others the joy of salvation through the precious blood of Christ. You have worked diligently in his vineyard in Japan. Why are results so difficult to come by? Let us examine barriers we are facing one by one.

You may remember from the fifties to the seventies there was a cartoon character called Pogo. He lived in the animal kingdom, loved nature, and nurtured a special blend of living philosophy. One day, walking in the forest, he came upon these immortal words: "Yep son, we have met the enemy and he is us."[1]

Sardonic, perhaps, but when we get in front of a mirror on the wall, we know Pogo is right. In everything we do, the greatest hindrance to our success comes from our own inadequacies and dispositions. Pogo reminds us that we must examine ourselves first before we approach others.

Let us be honest with ourselves. When we try to tell others about Christ, don't we sometimes have a notion that we are better

---

1. Commodore Oliver Hazard Perry's braggadocio, "We have met the enemy and they are ours," rendered during the War of 1812, might have been the source of inspiration for Walt Kelly, Pogo's creator. In this book, however, we will give Pogo full credit.

than they, because we know Christ? That is a dangerous attitude, because when we have that arrogance, our listeners will know it instantly.

Peter was a person just like us. The night he was betrayed, Jesus told his disciples: "All of you will be made to stumble because of me this night."

"Oh, no, not me," Peter was quick to protest. "Even if I have to die with you, I will not deny you." We all know what happened that night (Matt 26:31–33).

Hubris is a dangerous enemy. We make mistakes when we entertain a notion of our own self-importance. Ferdinand Magellan (1480–1521) was a great circumnavigator, but little is known of his work as a missionary, and it was in that capacity that he met his untimely death. In March 1521, his armada reached the shores of Cebu Island in the present-day Philippines. He staked a claim for his Christian Majesty, the King of Spain. Datum Huambo, ruler of the Cebu Island was baptized along with his followers. Magellan staged an Easter mass that dazzled them. He even succeeded in a miracle of faith healing that made the Filipinos passionate believers. Magellan was exuberant and tarried there to stage another miracle to see more Filipinos convert to Christ. To show his host the might of soldiers backed by the cross, he proposed to annihilate Huambo's enemy in the neighboring island without any help from the latter. His own captains pointed out the plan's folly. Magellan insisted on commanding a troop of forty-nine to face an enemy thirty times larger than his. He was feeling invincible and was burning with a missionary zeal. The plan was a total disaster. Soon thereafter Huambo backslid and expelled his remaining visitors. As a navigator, Magellan was patient and deliberate, but as an evangelist he was neither, hence his failure.

How can we avoid this pitfall called hubris? Jesus washed the feet of his disciples to teach them. "If I then, your Lord and Teacher, have washed your feet, you also ought to wash one another's feet' (John 13:14). In Jesus' times in Palestine, roads were not paved. They were likely strewn with human and animal excrement. Travelers wore sandals to trek on these roads. When they reached the inn, servants at the bottom of the totem pole were the ones to remove the sandals and wash their feet. That was exactly the task Jesus performed for his disciples. This lesson is simple yet profound; before we appear in front of others to lead them, we must submit ourselves completely to the Lord.

It is not easy to be a minister or a missionary. Yet deep in your heart you know that you have been ordained to serve others. It means that the needs of others must come first before your own. The word "minister" comes from the Greek word *diakonos* (διάκονος), which is a compound consisting of *dia* and *konos*. *Dia* means "completely," and *konos* means "dust." The word, thus combined, meant, "Run as fast as you can, let the dust rise on the road, go and serve others." This word is translated interchangeably as "minister" or "servant."

What must you do to become a proper *diakonos*? It is simple. You must be a good listener. For a minister or a missionary to succeed, the first lesson to learn is to listen. It is no accident that our creator has given us two ears and two eyes but only one mouth. Show your concern for those you serve by listening to their needs. They may not know the Bible as well as you do, and they may not have had as much education as you have, but their life experiences are very important to them and should be to you as well, who serve them. Follow the example set by our servant Messiah. Be ready to wash their feet. That will go a long way toward your own success.

Dr. James Curtis Hepburn (1815–1911), the first American protestant missionary to Japan, typified this faithful discipleship. In 1879, he published the first-ever Japanese-English dictionary, and finished translating the New Testament. "In literary skills and knowledge, my collaborators far surpass me," he wrote to a friend of his, "I only trudged along with perseverance. I praise our Lord for giving me this opportunity to serve him. *Soli Deo Gloria.*"[2] After this he went on to complete the translation of the Old Testament.

---

2. Letter, dated October 31, 1879, retranslated into English from Takaya Michio, tr. *Hebon no Tegami (Hepburn's Letters)* (Yokohama: Yurindo, 1976), 141.

Overcoming Barriers to Evangelization in Japan

The Japanese people had difficulty pronouncing Dr. Hepburn's name. It was shortened to Hebon, which he loved, because it sounded like the Japanese word *heibon*, which meant "just being ordinary." In Hepburn's days, Japanese society was highly structured and hierarchical even more so than today. Teachers were revered more than their own parents due to the Confucian tradition. In this, Hepburn departed from the norm. He insisted that his students were his fellow workers in the Lord's vineyard. He founded Meiji Gakuin University and Shiloh Church in Yokohama. He headed the former only briefly, allowing for just enough time to nurture a capable successor. His humility and willingness to let others take the lead were the keys to his success. His legacy in Japan endures.

Odds were against him when Hepburn reached the shores of Kanagawa in 1859. He was already forty-four years old and it was unlikely that he could acquire necessary language skills. The government was hostile to foreigners. Under their watchful eyes, he nevertheless managed to gain the services of a young Japanese physician to come to teach him Japanese.[3] He had some knowledge of *kanji* through his previous tour to China. Learning *kana*, and mostly through observation, he eventually attained fluency in the language. As a medical doctor he was allowed to maintain contact with ordinary people. It was through that contact he was able to know the language thoroughly. As a doctor, he patiently cured the sick, observed the people, and learned from them. Preaching to them came much later, since the ban on Christianity was not lifted until 1873.

Japan was a dangerous place to be for foreigners in the years between 1859 and 1868. The country was in turmoil. "Respect the emperor, expel the barbarians" was the battle cry of the forces that wanted to topple the Tokugawa government. An assassin entered Hepburn's home and injured his wife. Hepburn kept that to himself, for fear that reporting it might create a situation which would

---

3. From the very beginning of studying Japanese, a language so foreign to Westerners, Hepburn started keeping copious notes for the purpose of creating a Japanese-English dictionary. Letter, dated May 5, 1860, ibid., 60–66.

Barrier I: Self

force the American government to send expeditionary troops to protect the lives of its citizens.

Today we still have a lot of obstacles to conquer in order to bring the good news to Japan. However, compared to the difficulties Hepburn had to face, ours should not deter us. If barriers still look too formidable, it is time for us to take a good look at ourselves. Could it be that we have become defeatists, taking failure for granted? Could it also be that we have failed to recognize opportunities at every turn because we have forgotten to immerse ourselves into Japanese society?

Hudson Taylor (1832–1905), founder of the China Inland Mission (now OMF International), went to China wearing native Chinese clothing and trimming his hair Chinese style. He looked awkward and was scorned by many proper English gentlemen. What he wanted was to immerse body and soul into Chinese society. He set an example not easy to follow. Thus, please ask yourself this question: "Am I getting too comfortable in my job as a *gaijin* missionary?" If your answer is yes, that would be a danger sign. Let us work hard to prove our friend Pogo wrong.

Pogo is not alone in stressing the importance of self-reflection. The Ming Confucian scholar Wang Yang-ming's (1472–1529) dictum "It is easier to destroy a bandit in the mountain than destroying a bandit in one's own heart" says very much the same. This dictum was a favorite phrase cited by samurai while they trained to perfect their *bushido*. It was in a group of students trained in this philosophy that Leroy Lansing Janes (1838–1909) found thirty early converts to Christianity in 1874.[4] Janes was patient. He observed and listened to his students carefully for close to three years before teaching them the essence of Christianity. He appealed to their *bushido* sense of *noblesse oblige*. In today's parlance, Janes

---

4. This group, known as the Kumamoto Band, included Ebina Danjō (1856–1937), who as a minister and educator left an indelible mark on the development of Protestantism in Japan. On the Kumamoto Band, see Shuma Iwai, "Syncretism of Christian samurai at the Kumamoto Band in Japan: Fulfillment of Confucianism in Christianity," in *Religion on the Move!: New Dynamics of Religious Expansion in a Globalizing World*, edited by Afe Adogame and Shobana Shankar (Leiden: Brill, 2012), 113–32.

Overcoming Barriers to Evangelization in Japan

knew how to contextualize his message. A Civil War artillery officer, Janes spoke the language of warriors who counted among their virtues self-denial and self-reflection.

Janes's experience provides an important lesson for all of us who have been educated in the Western tradition. Our thought process has been governed by the Aristotelian logic, and our systematic theology has been structured to appeal to our collective rational mind. Thus when we try to reach out to our Japanese friends with our carefully constructed doctrine, we cannot understand why they could not accept its logical message. We quickly condemn them as still living in darkness. But fault is actually on our side, because we have never taken seriously the unassailable fact that there is a limit to the Aristotelian logic in guiding our daily lives.

When we talk to our children, we want it to be from heart to heart, and logic always takes a back seat. Jesus did not rely on Aristotelian logic. He used parables to instruct his disciples. Janes's success came from his humility and from his willingness to listen to his students. In the end, he was able to touch their hearts, which resulted in the historic mass conversion.

In this book, I have avoided raising theological issues, but have relied on a case-by-case study of barriers which have prevented our Japanese friends from accepting Christ. Please step into their shoes to see why it has been so difficult for them to discard their old ways. It may give you a moment of self-reflection to discover a new way of approaching your Japanese friends.

So far I have been urging you to engage in self-refection. Once you have mastered this art of self-reflection, I hope you will share your understanding and skills with your entire Japanese congregation. The church, as a corporate body of Christ, must cast away its own hubris. Are we as a church too self-content and self-absorbing? Are we so self-righteous that we drive away people from joining our church? The question of self as a barrier applies equally to church as a corporate body. I shall return to this subject in chapter 7.

Barrier I: Self

In the following chapters, the issue of contextualization will be discussed. We must take into account the richness of Japan's traditional culture, and pay due respect to it. If we go to Japan only to condemn its culture's darkness, our mission will invariably fail.[5]

You may have been in Japan a long time, or you may have just stepped on the shores of Japan. Either way I know you are eager to share your knowledge of the gospel with your Japanese friends. May I make one suggestion? Before you do anything else, please try to make a mental note that the Japanese people you will meet are going to become your teachers about their own society.[6] Let them show you who they are, what their likes and dislikes are, and learn from them how to reach others. When you meet Christian friends, get to know them, and as your friendship grows deeper, ask them how they became Christians. There are some who are

---

5. Shoki Coe (1914–1988), a Cambridge-trained Taiwanese theologian, was the first one to pose the issue of contextualization. He was aware of the danger of producing a chameleon theology that simply changed the message of the gospel to fit with the context. That is not the approach we will be taking in Japan. Neither will we compromise the catholicity of the gospel that Christ died for our sins on the cross. In the above paragraph, I have stressed the importance of paying respect to Japan's traditional culture. This is consistent with Coe's original intent of advocating contextualization. In 1948, he was the keynote speaker at the Summer Youth Christian Convention in Taiwan. Facing assembled foreign missionaries, he urged them to use the word "contextualization," since the word "indigenization" was often used pejoratively by missionaries to look down on the native cultures. "Please respect our culture," he said. "In its richness you see very few equals." It was an electrifying moment for the convention. As one of the attendees, I can attest to the excitement. It was the first time ever that any Taiwanese had dared to speak out on equal terms with foreign missionaries. Coe went on to become director of the theological education fund of the World Council of Churches. The word "contextualization" came in vogue in the seventies. See Ray Wheeler, "The Legacy of Shoki Coe," *International Bulletin of Missionary Research* 26.2 (2002) 77–80. journals.sagepub.com/doi/abs/10.1177/239693930202600205.

6. In this you will be following the tradition set by Confucius, and it will please your Japanese friends. "When walking in a party of three, I always have teachers. I can select the good qualities of the one for imitation, and the bad ones of the other and correct them in myself." *Analects of Confucius* VII:21. From *Sources of Chinese Tradition* by William Theodore de Bary (New York: Columbia University Press, 1960), 25. Reprinted with permission of the publisher.

second- or third-generation Christians, but they are still in the minority. You will find that some of them have been disowned by their families because they became Christians. You will find others who have either come from Buddhist or Shinto families, and they are still familiar with those pagan practices. You will also find that many Christians are married to non-Christian spouses. The issue of mixed marriage, just raised, will be discussed extensively in the next chapter. It is one of the major factors in the Christian community losing members instead of gaining. Without further ado, let us now look into the reasons why Buddhism has such a strong sway over the Japanese public.

Chapter 2

Barrier II
Buddhism Enmeshed in Japanese Culture

BUDDHISM IS AN INTEGRAL part of Japanese culture. In Japanese literature, arts, and in the language itself, one cannot escape the influence of Buddhism.

There is a haiku posted in the Horyuji temple in Nara:

Kaki kueba	Eating persimmon
Kane ga narunari	Sound of gong
Horyuji	Horyuji

Typical of a haiku, this poem is one of utter simplicity. Yet in it you will find love of nature, appreciation for the changing of the seasons, and in this case one's religious sentiment, all compressed into seventeen syllables. Autumn is when persimmons are ripe and sweet. One hears the sound of a gong from a distance. Oh, it must be from Horyuji! The poet's mind wanders back to the glory days of old when the most ancient of this structure was built in 607.

This haiku is by Meiji-period poet Masaoka Shiki (1867–1902). I have chosen this haiku to start this chapter because it is vintage Japanese. To a foreigner it may not say much, but to the Japanese, it instantly binds them to their common cultural heritage that was nurtured by Buddhism through the ages.

Overcoming Barriers to Evangelization in Japan

You can also find this sentiment in *The Tale of Genji*, the earliest work of fiction completed in the early eleventh century; *The Tale of Heike* that chronicled the rise and fall of the Taira clan; Matsuo Basho's immortal haiku travelogue, *The Narrow Road of Oku;* and in many other works of Japanese literature.

Buddhism set the standards for beauty in many areas. The Japanese garden, whose simple design expresses a specific worldview, is one such instance. Japanese painting and calligraphy are others. The tea ceremony was developed in a Zen monastery, and so was Ikebana, the art of flower arrangement.

In their daily lives, the influence of Buddhism is also pervasive. *Obon* is a three-day festival held in mid-summer to honor the souls of ancestors. It is the time for many to return to their ancestral homes to tend the graves. In the process it creates some of the worst traffic congestion in the nation. Gifts are exchanged as *Ochugen*, and life goes on.

How did Buddhism, an alien religion, come to hold such an important place in Japanese culture? In today's parlance, it was able to contextualize its messages and nurture leaders from the ranks of indigenous believers. Here is a quick overview.[1]

Nara (710–784) and pre-Nara Periods: Buddhism reached the shores of Japan in 552 by way of Korea. It was a belief system that claimed to have a magical power which would protect a nation. This brand of Buddhism was first developed in China when that country was divided into several contending kingdoms. It was this aspect of Buddhism that attracted the attention of the ruling clans of Japan. The imperial clan was one of many contending with each

---

1. If you are pressed for time, you can skip this historical survey, and go directly to "How to Approach Buddhism and Buddhists" on page 18 for practical steps to be taken. However, be sure to return to this survey when you have time. It is important to have this knowledge, so you can have meaningful conversations with your Buddhist friends.

Barrier II: Buddhism Enmeshed in Japanese Culture

other. Its embrace of Buddhism was followed by the clan's victory. In return, it became a sponsor and protector of Buddhism in Japan.

Embracing Buddhism proved to be a wise political move for the imperial clan and other great families. Japan was still in her formative stage. Previously there was no cohesive political structure that could bind people together beyond familial ties. China, reunited under the Sui Dynasty in 581 and followed by the Tang Dynasty in 618, was experiencing the golden age of her civilization. Her well-structured government ruled a vast area seamlessly. Japan had much to learn from China. Buddhism provided the vehicle for the importation of Chinese civilization. Many of the monks, who were well-educated transplants from the continent, served as intermediaries.

In 752, exactly 200 years after the arrival of Buddhism, the great Buddha in Nara was completed. A ceremony to commemorate its completion was attended by representatives from the then-known world. It signified that Japan had come of age, entering the rank of the "advanced" nations. At the same time, state-sponsored temples were built in the capitals of all provinces. Buddhism became, in effect, the official religion of the nation.

There was no evidence to suggest that Buddhism had penetrated the hearts and souls of ordinary Japanese people at this stage. Common people were definitely out of Buddhism's reach. If they had an occasion to observe Buddhist ceremonies they were dazzled by their magical power and splendor. Their doctrine was mysterious and hard to understand. It had no sway over people's daily lives.

A pattern for Buddhism's success emerged. It provided the services that the state required. Monks provided intellectual and technical manpower. Whatever they suggested in the name of Buddha worked well. It was magic in the eye of its beholder. In return, Buddhist temples received generous donations from the imperial court and major clans.

Power corrupted these temples, and one monk even attempted to usurp the throne. To escape those corrosive influences of powerful temples, Emperor Kammu moved the capital first to Nagaoka, and then on to Heiankyo.

Heian Period (794-1195): The moving of the capital to present-day Kyoto ushered in an era of genuinely Japanese cultural development. Influence from the continent remained strong, but people learned to became more selective. In the process, it created a cultural norm which was separate from that of the continent. The main players in this process were court nobles whose leisure time allowed them to engage in variegated pursuits of arts and literature. New sects of Buddhism were formed, reflecting this cultural trend.

Two monks, Saicho (767-822) and Kukai (774-835), accompanied the Japanese embassy to Tang China in 804. Saicho remained there eight months to study and then returned home to establish the Tendai sect. Kukai remained in China three years before returning home to establish the Shingon sect. These two events marked the beginning of Japanese Buddhism that distinguished itself from other forms of Buddhism practiced in China and India.

The masters of these new sects were not those who came from the continent. Being natives of Japan, they were willing to make accommodations to traditional Shinto deities. Saicho built a monastery in Mt. Hiei overlooking the capital city from the northeast. In this way, he paid tribute to the Shinto deity, Sanno, or King of the Mountains. Shingon's basic doctrine claimed that all Buddhas and Bodhisattvas were manifestations of the Supreme Buddha. Kukai took this one step further to argue that all Shinto deities were manifestations of the Supreme Buddha.

Mt. Hiei's monastery became the center of Buddhist learning, where generations of Buddhist priests were trained. In a country where there was no other institution of higher learning, it became the university par excellence. At its height there were 3,000 buildings in its complex that housed thousands of aspiring priest scholars. In later years, various other sects of Buddhism would emerge in Japan. Most of their founders received their first training at Mt.

Barrier II: Buddhism Enmeshed in Japanese Culture

Hiei. This example was followed closely by Zen temples. In Japan's Middle Ages, five Zen temples in Kyoto competed to be recognized as the top-ranked institution of higher learning. These institutions served both religious and secular purposes.

The Shingon sect's impact was mostly felt in Japanese art. The tantric belief system originating from India was too complex to transfer to Japan. Instead of conveying that system in words, Kukai chose rituals and various art forms, including pictures as well as calligraphy. In the early Heian period, Japan still did not have its own writing system, and used Chinese characters to transcribe Japanese words and pronunciation. The *kana* system, an equivalent of the Western alphabet, was developed by monks trying to translate Buddhist scriptures into Japanese. More likely than not, this process was started in a Shingon monastery.

Like Saicho, Kukai chose to build his temple on a mountain top in Mt. Koya, fifty miles south of the capital and away from temptations of the secular world. It was there he was buried. The place became a place of choice for the nobility to place their own remains, believing that they would be sharing the merits of Kukai in their afterlives. Today it is a historic site. More notable Japanese were buried there than in any other cemetery in all of Japan. Buddhism at this stage remained a religion for the nobility. Temples did engage in charitable works, but they were of limited scope and reached only a small number.

Around the turn of the millennium there was an outcry that the Latter Degenerate Days *(mappo)* were at hand. Buddha entered nirvana 1,500 years earlier. During the following five centuries his Right Law, informed by the light of his teachings, reigned. It was mankind's golden age of peace and prosperity. The next five centuries were an era of his Reflected Law. The light of his teachings no longer shone directly, but its reflections were sufficient to keep the world in peace. Buddhist believers feared that the light shone by Buddha and its reflections were about to be extinguished. The end of the world was near. There were many signs to abet their fears. In Japan the nobility had lost their grip over the nation. No power strong enough had emerged to take their place. The new land-tenure system called *shoen* further complicated the matter. The rights of those who cultivated the land were far more restricted than before. Disturbances were everywhere. The two established sects, Tendai and Shingon, were unable to answer the needs of this changing world.

What emerged was a slow process of reformation in Japanese Buddhism. It was a reformation with a lower case r. To avoid the danger presented by the Latter Degenerate Days, they reasoned that it was necessary to return to the original doctrine of Buddha. Spearheading these reform movements was the monk Genshin (942–1017). In his *Essentials for Salvation*, he depicted the horrors of hell and contrasted them vividly with the bliss of the Western Paradise. To attain rebirth in this paradise, Genshin stressed faith in the efficacy of the original vow of Amida Buddha. To demonstrate their faith, people were taught to say *nembutsu*, reciting the sacred name of Amida with a chant *"namu amidabutsu"* (Hail to the glorious name of Amida Buddha).

By stressing faith and dependence on the power of another (*tariki*), Genshin brought a totally new concept to Japanese Buddhism. It denied, as a means of salvation, dependence on one's own power (*jiriki*). It was the faith of each individual that mattered, not ascetic observances, spiritual and metaphysical exercises, or the good works that the priestly class advocated. In this way, Genshin opened the gate of paradise to common men.

Kamakura Period (1185–1333): In 1185 the Bakufu[2] was established in Kamakura and this little seaside village in the Kanto area became the effective seat of power for the next 148 years. It represented the Japanese people's movement eastward which eventually would make the Kanto plain the center of the nation. Power was no longer in the hands of effeminate court nobles, but in the hands of pragmatic and action-minded warriors. The country was ripe for creating a new culture consistent with their

---

2. An administrative structure headed by the *shogun*. Technically the *shogun* was named to that post by the emperor, but in reality he exercised full administrative power over the entire nation.

Barrier II: Buddhism Enmeshed in Japanese Culture

worldviews. The energy of this new era had a profound effect on the religious reform movement.[3] New sects formed during this period brought Buddhism closer to the common people, and as such they continue to influence people's daily lives today. Let us take a quick look at some of the major sects.

True Pure Land Sect: Following Genshin, Honen (1133–1212) advocated the absolute efficacy of *nembutsu* and became the founder of the Pure Land (Jodo) Sect. Shinran (1173–1262) followed the same teachings, but differed from Honen on one aspect. For Honen, the awakening of faith required diligent observance of prayers to the Three Treasures. Thus there was still an element of acquiring faith by one's own power. To Shinran faith is a gift freely given by all the Buddhas, and it was by faith alone that would bring salvation. After his death, Shinran's followers were organized into a new sect calling themselves the True Pure Land Sect (Jodo Shin Shiu or simply Shin Shiu). They were divided into two wings, East and West, following the names of their headquarter temples. Together they constitute the most dominant Buddhist sect today.

The Pure Land faith appealed to farmers, city dwellers, and other common people. Some samurai also became devotees of this faith. However, samurai were by upbringing and training self-reliant and could not always find themselves comfortable in the teachings which stressed dependence on another's power. The newly formed Rinzai and Soto sects of Zen provided the answer.

Zen Buddhism: The word "Zen" is a Japanese rendition of the Chinese term *chan*, which in turn is derived from the Sanskrit *dhyana*, meaning "meditation." While the doctrine is inspired by early Buddhist precepts, Zen is a peculiarly East Asian product; it contains the mystic tradition of Taoism, is infused to a lesser

---

3. See David Lu, *Japan: A Documentary History* (New York: M. E. Sharpe, 1997), 117–45, for a capsule description of these sects and excerpts from their writings.

Overcoming Barriers to Evangelization in Japan

extent with pragmatic Confucian teachings, both of which are blended together with Buddhist ideals. In later Tang and Song periods, there were seven schools of Zen in China that constituted a potent intellectual current. Two of these schools were brought back to Japan by Eisai (1141–1215) and Dogen (1200–1253) to become the Rinzai and Soto sects.

It is the Zen belief that every individual has a Buddha-nature within him, and it is not necessary to go outside of oneself to discover the Buddha nature. Introspection and self-understanding, rather than scriptural or other external authorities, are the keys to enlightenment. Truth can be known if one's mind is cleansed of old habits and prejudices. Added to this is a rigorous application of meditation, through which mind must be permitted to make its own discovery. To this end, different methods have been devised, and two are still in use today. One is *koan* or "public theme" which consists of a question and an answer between the master and his disciple.

Another widely used method is *zazen* or "sitting in meditation." Both Eisai and Dogen stressed the importance of *zazen*, but the latter did so by minimizing the importance of *koan*. Unlike *koan*, "sitting in meditation" means without any specific problem in mind and without any thought for achieving enlightenment. Thus there is a sense of self-abatement.

Zen taught the value of introspection, tight discipline, and self-reliance, which found favor among the samurai. By teaching the possibility of sudden enlightenment, without waiting for the moment of death, they also gave a new meaning to the life to be lived on this earth.

Zen priests maintained close contact with the Southern Song and became agents for importing the latter's cultural attainments, such as the new style of painting. Tea was brought back to Japan by Eisai. That created the tradition of the tea ceremony which is now closely identified with Japanese culture. Zen's legacy in Japan is multifold. Five major Zen temples in Kyoto became major centers of learning. Some modern philosophical schools of thought can be traced back to these schools. For a long period of time, Zen monks

Barrier II: Buddhism Enmeshed in Japanese Culture

were found in government services and in trade negotiations with China.

The Nichiren Sect: Another Buddhist tradition which developed in the Kamakura period was the sect begun by Nichiren (1222–1282). Nichiren received his training at Mt. Hiei and also studied Jodo and Zen doctrines. Finding all of them wanting, he came to the conclusion that only the *Lotus Sutra* contained the true doctrine, and if that sutra could be propagated, the world could yet be saved from the turmoil of the Latter Degenerate Days. His watch words were *namu horengekyo*, or "hail to the glory of the Lotus Sutra." He was the first thinker to claim the unique position held by Japan in Buddhism. Buddhism was begun in India and transmitted to China and then on to Japan. But it was in Japan that the true and superior teaching was maintained, he asserted.

Initially Nichiren attracted samurai as his adherents, but gradually farmers and merchants came into his fold. His militant messages gave voice and solace to the farmers and merchants who were suppressed by the samurai class. The tradition which was set at that time is continued today. In fact both the Soka Gakkai and Rissho Koseikai, the two militant Buddhist groups in contemporary Japan, trace their origins to Nichiren's teachings. Their believers come mainly from lower-middle-class people who do not share fully in the current economic prosperity. The superior organization, cultural events, militant pronouncements, and self-assertiveness these groups provide give voice to the disenchanted and create a sense of belonging.

Knowledge of Kamakura Buddhism is essential in order to serve well in Japan. First of all, the landscape of Buddhism today closely follows the pattern set in the Kamakura period, and many Japanese families can trace their ancestry and belief systems back to that period. In your conversations with them, if you know which sect they are from: the Shin, the Nichiren, or one of the Zen sects, the contents of your talk can change dramatically. Secondly, today we speak of contextualization. As described above, Buddhists

Overcoming Barriers to Evangelization in Japan

were quite adept at it, but often at the cost of changing their basic teachings. We, of course, do not have that freedom, nor would we want it. But we can reflect on what the Buddhists did, and with ever-increasing knowledge of Japanese civilization we can explore the question: "To what extent can we contextualize Christianity to Japanese culture today?"

We shall stop our brief survey now. But there are a few more points I must make before I leave this subject. First, Buddhism could not have attained its dominant position in Japan without the support of those who were in power, whether it was from the imperial court, great clan chiefs, or the Shogun. Their donations gave the temples financial support to allow them to prosper. In return the temples provided services to the state and its other sponsors. There were a few exceptions to this formula. Oda Nobunaga (1534–1582), in his quest to unify the country, burnt down the entire Mt. Hiei complex and killed off its monk soldiers in 1571. When the new Meiji government was formed in 1868, it allowed a movement to discard Buddha and destroy his statues (*Haibutsu Kishaku*). It was an attempt to destroy the symbiotic relations that existed between various sects of Buddhism and the Bakufu during the Edo period (1603–1867), about which I shall discuss in due course. It is important to remember that the imperial family has consistently maintained close ties with Buddhism. Many emperors' graves can be found in Kyoto temples. In the Sennyuji temple alone, sixteen emperors were buried. In the waning days of the Pacific War, Prince Konoye Fumimaro, a pre-war prime minister, attempted to hide Emperor Showa in the Ninnaji temple as a priest, for fear that he might be indicted as a war criminal.

HOW TO APPROACH BUDDHISM AND BUDDHISTS

The *2018 Report of Japan's Religious Population*[4] shows that 47.1 percent of Japanese people are Buddhists as compared to 1.1 percent Christians, which include Catholics as well as evangelicals. As

---

4. http://www.bunka.go.jp/tokei_hakusho_shuppan/hakusho_nenjihokokusho/shukyo_nenkan/pdf/h30nenkan_gaiyo.pdf, 3.

Barrier II: Buddhism Enmeshed in Japanese Culture

a missionary you are trying to help this minority of 1.1 percent to face the 47 percent and try to bring them to Christ. Odds are against you. But how can it be done? First, try to find opportunities to have conversations with Buddhists. Second, seek help from members of your congregation (or those Japanese believers with whom you have been in contact) who are married to non-Christians. Get a Japanese partner and work as a team. Remember always, be a good listener. They will think that you are a good conversationalist even when you may not feel comfortable with your Japanese.

CONVERSATIONS WITH PRIESTS AND NUNS

There are some Buddhists who have chosen to become priests and nuns. Respect their choice, and do not doubt their faith. They have chosen the same way you have done as a Christian to become a pastor. Only they have chosen a different god. Try to find some points of contact with them and learn from them. If the occasion calls for, you can even suggest to a Zen priest, "Well I will be happy to come to your temple for *zazen*, and I will like you to visit my church in return." It is not a sacrilege to sit in meditation because, as discussed earlier, *zazen* is not an act of worshiping Buddha.

Paul the apostle, who was a great missionary, will support this step you take. "For though I am free from all men, I have made myself a servant to all, that I might win the more; and to the Jews I became a Jew, that I might win Jews; to those who are under the law, as under the law, that I might win those who are under the law." (1 Cor 9:19–20) To lead your Buddhist friends to Christ, you must immerse yourself into their midst to understand them. Once that step is taken a serious conversation can begin.

The Rev. Uemura Masahisa (1858–1925) was an early convert to Christianity who became a major voice in the Christian community in the Meiji era. In 1911, he wrote an article suggesting that the saving grace exhibited by Amida Buddha reminded him of imputation as taught by Calvin. He then noted that Christians should learn from the faith expressed by Honen and Shinran.[5] Professor Yanaihara Tadao (1893–1961), forced to resign from Tokyo University because of his opposition against Japanese militarism, was a Christian leader who wrote a number of Bible commentaries. Among the four people he admired most, he cited the name of Shinran because the faith he expressed was akin to Luther's *sola fide*. Here I would like to cite from Shinran's *Tannisho*:

> We proclaim: "If a good man can attain salvation, even more so a wicked man," However, most people in this world will say, "If a wicked man can attain salvation, even more so a good man." This latter statement seems reasonable on the surface, but it is against the spirit of our belief in the efficacy of the Original Vow. Let me explain. The man who is depending on his own power to do good is lacking in his aspiration to depend on another's power, and is led astray from the Original Vow of Amida Buddha. However, if he repents of his desire to depend on his own power and becomes solely reliant on Amida, he can then attain salvation in the True Land of Recompense."[6]

This is a beautiful confession of faith which always reminds me of the thief on the cross with Christ:

> Then one of criminals who were hanged blasphemed him, saying, 'If You are the Christ, save Yourself and us.' But the other, answering, rebuked him, saying, 'Do you not even fear God, seeing you are under the same condemnation? And indeed justly, for we receive the due reward of our deeds, but this Man has done nothing wrong.' Then he said to Jesus, 'Lord, remember me when You come into Your kingdom.' And Jesus said to him, 'assuredly, I say to you, today you will be with me in Paradise.' (Luke 23:39–43)

I once had a discussion with a True Pure Land sect priest on this issue that lasted nine hours, from three in the afternoon to

---

5. Takeda Kiyoko, *Kirisutokyo* (*Christianity*) (Tokyo: Chikuma Shobo, 1964), 15.

6. Lu, *Japan*, 135.

Barrier II: Buddhism Enmeshed in Japanese Culture

midnight. We both rejoiced in the fact that both of us had a similar understanding of what faith is all about. That long session gave me a chance to talk to him about redemption and God's plan of salvation. His commitment to Amida's original vow was genuine and enlightening. We were able to come jointly to the conclusion that no matter how great he was, Amida remained one of the many Buddhas. Therefore he was not absolute. In Christianity there was only one son of God, and he is absolute. *Solus Christus*!

As a missionary, I hope you will diligently seek opportunities to have conversations with your Japanese Buddhist friends. Listen to them carefully, and try to kindle their curiosity about Christianity. Always remember that God created them and planted in their minds seeds of knowing him. We all share his general revelation and common grace. Stress this common heritage before gradually leading them to his special revelation.

CONVERSATIONS WITH BUDDHIST PARISHIONERS

Unlike Christian churches, Buddhist temples do not have a Sunday worship service. Priests may give talks and advertise them, but they are not always given on a weekly basis. Parishioners may visit the temple on the anniversary dates of their departed ones to tend their graves, but otherwise they do not have any formal contact with the temple. Some temples have experimented with Sunday school, but it is normally poorly attended. Thus it will not be easy for anyone to find ways of making contact with Buddhist parishioners.

I was in Kyoto for a year and a half and made a practice of visiting as many temples as possible. While there I found one constant: many of the temples had their own tea ceremony or *ikebana* schools, and they were well attended by townspeople (and not tourists.)

Can we not do the same in our churches? my suggestion is for our churches to set up tea ceremony or *ikebana* schools of our own, to attract those people who may otherwise go to Buddhist temples for the same reasons. There may be resistance among our own people due to their Zen origin, but it is time for us to regard them as Japan's common cultural heritage divorced from Buddhism. Today, for example, none of us will reject a Christmas tree in our own home or church as it is fully integrated into our culture, and yet its origin was as a form of pagan nature worship.

Conversely some Japanese purists may argue that tea ceremonies and *ikebana* have to be performed in *tatami* rooms, but when these art forms were first introduced to the Western world, they were performed without *tatami*. Our churches can provide the much-needed space. Our most important consideration is to find a means of attracting Buddhist friends who are receptive to gospel messages. Let us co-opt their art forms. Why not give it a try?

BASIC TENETS OF BUDDHISM

Before we engage in conversation with our Buddhist friends, let us take a quick look at their belief system.

Like all other religions that emerged from India, Buddhism teaches that all beings are bound by a chain of causation, or karma. Life goes on forever, transmigrating from one form to another. The goal for a man is to be released from this chain of causation and enter into nirvana, to become one with the ultimate (*Atman*) where there is no more pain or suffering. In speaking of transmigration, one's status in the next life is determined by the actions of his present life. If he has acquired sufficient merit, he is guaranteed a better one in the next; if he has done poorly he may be reborn into another form.

Gautama Buddha lived around 500 BC and taught that (1) life is painful, (2) pain is caused by desire, (3) to remove pain, one must remove desire, and (4) to do so one must follow the teachings of Buddha. It was a simple message that stood against the cumbersome doctrine of Brahmanism of his time. Becoming a Buddhist was also made simple; all one has to do was recite the Three Treasures: "I follow Buddha, I follow his teachings, and I follow his monastic order."

Barrier II: Buddhism Enmeshed in Japanese Culture

Over the years, Buddhism developed into two major schools of Mahayana and Theravada, and then went on to form various sects. The plethora of their doctrines is impossible to summarize, and yet in spite of all their differences, there are three statements which they have in common. They are: "Impermanence of things," "No self in all laws," and "Everything is painful."

"Impermanence of things" is the phrase that has captured the imagination of generations of Japanese. It is contained in the first paragraph of the immortal work of literature, *The Tale of Heike*. The theme of impermanence runs through all great literary works. There is a phrase *mono no aware*, or the "intrinsic sadness of things," to describe Japanese sensitivity to beauty. Beauty is one thing that is passing, and every piece of art has as its goal capturing that evanescent moment.

"No self in all laws" is a teaching that one must deny himself in search of nirvana. The goal of *zazen*, for example, is one of total self-abatement.

"Everything is painful" is the phrase that described living conditions in ancient India well. It requires little elaboration. Its worldview is negative toward life on this earth. Let us cite a passage from the Bible to contrast it with our views:

> Rejoice in the Lord always. Again I will say, rejoice! Let your gentleness be known to all men. The Lord is at hand. Be anxious for nothing, but in everything by prayer and supplication, with thanksgiving, let your request be known to God, and the peace of God, which surpasses all understanding, will guard your hearts and minds through Christ Jesus. (Phil 4:4–7)

In a similar vein, let us examine a few more of Buddhism's basic teachings.

Transmigration: There is no comparable doctrine in Christianity. Buddhism does not deal with creation or how life began. Man is not unique, he is but one of many beings with whom he is bound closely with the chain of karma.

In contrast we know that there was a beginning for us and for the world we live in. "In the beginning God created the heavens and the earth" (Gen 1:1). We do not interchange our lives with other creatures, and we live on this earth but once. "And as it is appointed for men to die once, but after this the judgment" (Heb 9:27). We have a totally different worldview from our Buddhist brothers. Our salvation does not hinge on the good works we are supposed to accumulate through transmigration of our lives.

Nirvana: In the west, "nirvana" has become a synonym of "ecstasy" or "sublime happiness." It implies that there is a "self" behind that ecstasy. That is not what Buddhism teaches. Nirvana is absolute nothingness. There is no sound of music for any individual to enjoy in this total void. Nirvana is the final release from the chain of causation, from those painful migrations to the next life. (The self with its desires is gone.) In this respect, nirvana is not a paradise or heaven, nor is it eternity. The *summum bonum* for Buddhists is the release from life itself: a final extinction; an obliteration of the person who labored through many karmic states saddled with those desires that caused pain.[7]

In contrast, Christianity teaches that life is a precious gift from God and that each individual is a unique creation of God. Life is not an illusion that can be blown away like a lit candle (but that could describe nirvana). Man lives under his grace alone (*sola gratia*) and for his glory alone (*soli Deo gloria*). The Bible teaches us that pain does not come from desire, but from the brokenness of the world caused by sin. Christians understand that they are born with sin and that sin separates them from a holy God, which means they are separated from both joy and their true purpose. This separation from God is the cause of the pain in life, but the truly good news is that this separation was eliminated in the work of Jesus Christ on the cross (*solus Christus*):[8]

---

7. There is a danger in jumping to the conclusion that Buddhism is nihilistic. Many missionaries have made this mistake and missed a chance to reach them effectively. If you study Buddhist scriptures, you will find that the path to enlightenment they teach contains many useful suggestions on how to conduct one's daily life.

8. Dealing with nirvana would be a good sermon topic. It will appeal to the Christian half of mixed couples who will take this message home to their Buddhist spouses.

Barrier II: Buddhism Enmeshed in Japanese Culture

And this is eternal life, that they may know you, the only true God, and Jesus Christ whom you have sent. (John 17:3)

Western Paradise and hell: Buddha's original teachings had no mention of paradise or hell, and this notion did not enter Japan until Genshin, as earlier described. Yet in these Jodo beliefs, we find similarities with our own notions of heaven and hell. It must also be noted that Shinran's attitude was one of *sola fide*, except that Shinran's notion of salvation depended on Amida Buddha, who is not an absolute figure. When this comparison is raised, it poses some challenge to Christians. So let us look into this issue a little further.

Salvation through faith advocated by Genshin and Shinran lit the fire of Buddhist revival, because it was able to answer the desperate needs of those who were worried about the imminence of the end of the world. It was against this "weariness of life" attitude that Kamakura Buddhism found a fertile ground to propagate its teachings.

Today's Japan provides an eerily similar landscape to that of one millennium earlier. From the pinnacle of "Japan as number one," its economy plunged into "the lost decade," from which it has yet to recover. Then there were the unprecedented natural disasters in Northeast Japan with a tsunami, loss of life, and a disabled nuclear plant. Pessimism, rampant in society, is reflected in the suicide rate. The *2016 White Paper on Suicide Prevention* shows that in comparing the suicide rate among 100,000 people as a unit, Japan registered as the sixth-worst in the world, and for women Japan was the third-worst. It is a serious societal problem as the society is also trying to find a way to solve its continuously lowering of the birth rate.[9]

Here is a challenge for you, as a missionary, to tackle. Use your imagination to find a solution to this problem. Why not engage your Buddhist friends as allies to solve this problem jointly?

---

9. *Mainichi Sinbin*, May 19, 2017. https://mainichi.jp/articles/20170519/k00/00m/040/187000c. For the full government text, see pages 75–77 of https://www.mhlw.go.jp/wp/hakusyo/jisatsu/17/dl/2-3.pdf.

Overcoming Barriers to Evangelization in Japan

As noted earlier, the apostle Paul would approve of this approach. Work diligently with your Buddhist friends to prevent suicide from occurring. In the latter part of this book I will suggest that churches set up counseling centers. With or without them, let your Buddhist counterparts have their say in how they will approach suicide prevention from their religious perspective. You can then share with them what we can offer.

The Heidelberg Catechism's first question, "What is your only comfort in life and death?," is answered as follows:

> That I am not my own, but belong with body and soul, both in life and in death, to my faithful Savior Jesus Christ. He has fully paid for all my sins with his precious blood, and has set me free from all the power of the devil. He also preserves me in such a way that without the will of my heavenly Father, not a hair can fall from my head; indeed, all things must work together for my salvation. Therefore, by his Holy Spirit he also assures me of eternal life and makes me heartily willing and ready from now on to live for him.[10]

This is in stark contrast to Jodo teachings. Believers in Amida could get their rewards in paradise, but only after death, whereas rewards for Christians are both on this earth as well as in heaven. This affirmation of our earthly life is the most potent message for suicide prevention. If you are working with your Buddhist friends, they can witness the difference. In the process, some of them may become convinced that they should also find solutions through Jesus. Please try this approach whenever you can. Your Buddhist co-workers could become followers of Christ, who in turn could become effective disseminators of the gospel among Buddhists in Japan.

---

10. "Heidelberg Cathechism, para. 5. https://students.wts.edu/resources/creeds/heidelberg.html.

Barrier II: Buddhism Enmeshed in Japanese Culture

BIBLE VS. BUDDHIST SCRIPTURES

Another stark difference can be found in what we consider as our basic sacred literature. The Old Testament consists of thirty-nine books, and the New Testament twenty-seven, for a total of sixty-six books. They can be bound in one volume, and that is the basic text adhered to by Catholics, Orthodox, Evangelicals, and all other Protestant denominations.

Buddhism does not have a strict standard to determine which book can be considered a sacred text. The most reliable compendium of Buddhist texts was compiled in Japan between 1924 and 1932 and published as *Taishō Revised Tripiṭaka* in 100 volumes. It contains 2,920 books. The texts for Mahayana Buddhism exceed 600 books. *The Lotus Sutra* group is at their core, and it alone claims forty-two books and occupies four large volumes, each 1,000 pages in length in this publication. There are 151 books in the Āgama *Sutra* group containing Buddha's original teachings. They were created over the years between the fourth and first century BC. As historical documents, they cannot match the accuracy that the four gospels can claim of being the documents assembled close to the times of Christ.

CHRISTIANS LIVING IN THE BUDDHIST WORLD

As your ministry in Japan progresses, you will find that there are many instances of intermarriage between Christians and Buddhists. It poses problems on one end, but creates great opportunities for us at the other end.

If the husband or wife is a nominal Buddhist, problems may not arise in their lives. The family's peace may be interrupted, however, when a relative comes to visit and questions "What happened to your Buddhist altar?" When it comes to the issue of how to raise the children, problems can intensify. There is a need for understanding between the husband and wife, whether or not the children can be sent to Sunday school and attend church services with the one believing parent.

Overcoming Barriers to Evangelization in Japan

When one party is a devout Buddhist, problems can intensify. He or she may want to have the children brought up in his/her own faith. It can sow a seed of discord between the husband and wife.

How do you counsel the couple in this situation? As much as we want Christianity to triumph, my first response is to counsel patience, for "love suffers long and is kind: love does not envy; love does not parade itself; is not puffed up; does not behave rudely; does not seek its own; is not provoked" (1 Cor 13:4). Love with patience remains the best weapon for bringing the nonbelieving partner to Christ.

Your counseling should also include the assurance given by Paul: "For the unbelieving husband is sanctified by the wife, and the unbelieving wife is sanctified by the husband; otherwise your children would be unclean, but now they are holy" (1 Cor 7:14). With this you must also give an admonition that every effort must be made to bring the children to Christ.

In Japan there are many so-called mission schools, including secondary schools and universities, which were established by missionaries. They annually graduate around 500,000 students. They are exposed to Christian teachings, and some are baptized before their graduation. However, once they enter society and get married, most of them will lose their Christian identity. This loss of Christian identity is more prevalent among women who normally quietly follow the traditions of their husbands.

In Japan, people generally choose to be married in churches or Shinto shrines, but at death almost all will be buried in Buddhist temple grounds. In the struggle between religions, Christianity almost always ends up losing, because of the weight of this cultural tradition.

In a mixed marriage between a Christian and a Buddhist, choosing a place to be buried becomes a very serious issue. Let me illustrate this by an example set by my dear friend and mentor Kiuchi Nobutane (1899–1993).[11]

---

11. My reminiscences, written in Japanese, can be accessed at http://www.laijohn.com.

Barrier II: Buddhism Enmeshed in Japanese Culture

Mr. Kiuchi was a grandson of Iwasaki Yataro (1835–1885), founder of the Mitsubishi *zaibatsu*, and had two pre-war prime ministers as his uncles. In the post-war years, he served as an adviser to Prime Ministers Yoshida, Ikeda, and Sato. I became acquainted with him when I was writing a column for a Japanese weekly, *The World and Japan*. I was invited regularly to its editorial board meeting over which Mr. Kiuchi presided. He had a son about my age who died of cancer at the age of 55. After his son's death, he often invited me to join him in his business trips. I knew I was taking the place of his son and he became a father figure to me. One day, he asked me to meet him at a Tokyo hotel, not at the company office. As I entered his room, he asked his secretary to leave, and took both of my hands with his. His eyes were moist with tears. Then he spoke: "When my son died, he had one final request, 'Dad please accept Christ. So we can meet in heaven.' I have been thinking and thinking about this, but I cannot. As you may know I am the vice chairman of All Japan Buddhist Association that has members across the nation. If I became a Christian, I would be betraying their trust. my wife is a Christian. There is nothing which will please her more if I became one. But as I have told you, I cannot. We came to a compromise. We have agreed that if I die first, my wife will bury me as a Christian. However, if she dies first, I will bury her as a Buddhist. As a Christian, how do you feel about this arrangement?" Mrs. Kiuchi was a granddaughter of Fukuzawa Yukichi (1835–1901), founder of Keio University, and a major figure in the Meiji enlightenment that ushered in Japan's westernization.

The best solution would be for Mr. Kiuchi to follow the last wish of his son and become a Christian. Apparently Mr. Kiuchi was unable to honor his son's last wish and was perturbed by it. I responded timidly: "Sir, I have to hope that you will die first, because as a Christian you will receive the assurance of eternal life in Christ. You will indeed have a chance of seeing your son in heaven." That was the last I saw of him.

A year later when I was back in Tokyo, his secretary came to see me and gave me an update on Mr. Kiuchi's last days. Mr. Kiuchi

Overcoming Barriers to Evangelization in Japan

was baptized before his death. He thought it would be dishonest, if he were to be buried as a Christian without being baptized. When he approached his wife's minister, the latter rejected his request because he had never seen him in church before. But then Mr. Kiuchi sang "I know that my redeemer liveth," and spoke about the meaning of redemption. He knew the entire *Messiah* score back to back. He cited Mendelsohn's *Elijah*, and went on to speak about Isaiah. The minister relented. Mr. Kiuchi in his youth was a member of a choral group that sang these oratorios.

BUDDHISM AND ANCESTRAL GRAVES

Mr. Kiuchi's case is an exception. In most instances when the question of burial arises, Buddhism exercises its holding power. I know of a lady who has been going to church for decades, but refrains from being baptized because to do so would prevent her from being buried with her husband in his ancestral burial ground. Her husband's priest insisted on that. This is one potent weapon that Buddhism has used to keep thousands of Japanese in its hold. Let us examine how Buddhism acquired this power. It was an accident of history that was triggered by the Bakufu's proscription of Christianity centuries ago.

Francis Xavier reached the shores of Kagoshima in 1549. Jesuit missionaries who followed him gained adherents among major *daimyos*. Some of them might have done so to get an advantage in importing gun powder, but once they had embraced Christianity they were willing to donate choice real estate to build churches as demanded by the missionaries. It was this act that triggered the first wave of proscription against Christianity in 1587.[12] Toyotomi Hideyoshi (1537–1598) allowed commoners to remain Christians, but those who held a fief were forbidden to do so. He feared that Christianity was the vanguard of aggression by the Spaniards and Portuguese. Land donated to the churches could become footholds for these powers.

---

12. See, Lu, *Japan*, 196

Barrier II: Buddhism Enmeshed in Japanese Culture

The Tokugawa family was in power from 1600. The Bakufu in 1612 issued its first ban on Christianity for Nagasaki, and extended it nationwide two years later. In 1633, it started issuing edicts to close the country from the outside world, and in 1639 completed the process. To be a Christian was a capital offense. There was a peasant rebellion in Shimabara, lasting from 1637 to 1638. It was conducted in the name of Christ, and the peasants, warriors, and family members alike willingly died for their faith.[13]

Bakufu did not have a nationwide network of police presence to enforce its ban on Christianity. The *baku-han* system was a system of indirect rule, carefully crafted to maintain the balance between the Tokugawa family and its subordinate *daimyos*. The only available nationwide institution was a network of temples. Every village, no matter how small, had at least one temple in it. It was a matter of convenience and political expediency that the Bakufu looked upon this network as a tool of enforcing its ban on Christianity.

It was an ingenious device. Everyone, warriors and commoners alike, was required to carry a certificate of paper, identifying him as a parishioner of a particular temple (*terauke shomon*). This had the effect of making Buddhism into an official religion. Temples were also required to keep census records, subject to government inspection. In this way, temples became administrative subdivisions of the government. To avoid disputes among different sects and temples, the Bakufu, in 1655, issued an edict forbidding competition among temples to obtain new parishioners.[14] Even though the parishioner's right to choose a temple was preserved on paper, this edict had a reverse effect of taking away that right. A parishioner's life became one completely bound by his temple from birth to death. He paid his annual dues to the temple throughout his life, and in death would be buried with his ancestors in the plot assigned by the same temple. With the advent of the Meiji government in 1868, the status of Buddhism as an official religion

---

13. Lu. *Japan*, 220–25.
14. Lu, *Japan*, 219–220

Overcoming Barriers to Evangelization in Japan

was abolished. However, their stranglehold on people remained as keepers of ancestors' remains.[15]

Buddhist temples have kept records of their parishioners for more than four centuries, and in some cases much longer. For anyone in Japan who is interested in ancestor research, his first stop is always to his family temple. This fact alone creates an almost unshakable bond. Some in the younger generation may want to cut ties with their family temples, and remove their ancestral remains elsewhere. In such cases, exorbitant fees would be assessed by the temples. The amounts were always set at a level most families could not afford. In these negotiations temples always held the upper hand. Previously, we have discussed the Japanese people's preference to have their funerals performed by Buddhist priests. It may simply be by a force of habit, but the facts just described are certainly in play. Over the years, Buddhist temples have refined their messages to serve their parishioners. Let us give them credit for that. But funerals are also a business which provides a significant part of temples' income. They are well prepared to protect their business interests at all costs.

Temple business practices aside, lay Buddhists take their teachings about death very seriously. For example, at the age of 65, Inamori Kazuo, founder of Kyocera, entered a Zen temple to complete a regimen of training to become a lay priest (*tokudo shukke*) so he could devote his twenty remaining years of life to prepare for death. "I created a company which in the field of fine ceramics has no peer in the world. But it means nothing in the scheme of things about my own life. When I die, my soul will leave me to travel to the next world. I must be prepared for it."[16] In a way, Inamori

---

15. The importance of being buried with the ancestral remains is well demonstrated in Mishima Yukio's novel, *After the Banquet,* in which a restaurant owner falls madly in love with an aristocrat, fantasizing about the joy of being buried with him in his ancestral temple. It is based on a true story involving Japan's former foreign minister, Arita Hachiro (1884–1965).

16. From his speech delivered at the Naigai News Forum, as published in the *World and Japan Monthly* No. 1237, (February, 2014), 34, 48–50. Mr. Inamori, known for his charitable works, is a recipient of the Othmer Gold Medal for outstanding contributions to progress in science and chemistry.

Barrier II: Buddhism Enmeshed in Japanese Culture

echoes a sentiment expressed in Ecclesiastes 7:1, "A good name is better than precious ointment, and the day of death than the day of one's birth." Can we allow Buddhism to monopolize this issue?

It is a challenge. What steps can we take to help our Buddhist friends sever their ties from their temples?

The monk Saigyo (1118–1190) left a short poem that is familiar to generations of Japanese.

> Let me die when flowers are in full bloom
>
> In the month of spring when the moon is full

Handel wished to die on Good Friday. It was on April 14, 1759, a day after Good Friday that he took his final breath. Both Saigyo and Handel beautified death and looked forward to the life yet to come. Saigyo alluded to the joy of paradise with flowers and the moon, and Handel wished to die and be resurrected with Christ.

As mentioned earlier, desire for the Western Paradise can only be fulfilled through faith in Amida Buddha. He was, however, not an absolute figure. Handel's Lord was the Son of God who was and is absolute. It is this powerful message of Jesus on the cross and his resurrection that we must convey, "O Death, where is your sting? O Hades, where is your victory" (1 Cor 15:55)? Man dies only once, and the meanings of his life cannot be separated from his death. As Christians, we cannot allow Buddhism to be the religion of choice in dealing with the issue of death.

What does it mean to you personally to live and die with Christ? As a missionary, you may be asked by your Japanese friends this question. Be frank with them. If you have any doubt about it yourself, share that doubt with them in a serious and searching manner. Will you be able to share with them the joy of resurrection in Christ? Please keep the following biblical passages in mind:

> For to me, to live is Christ, and to die is gain. But if I live on in the flesh, this will mean fruit from my labor, yet what I shall choose I cannot tell. For I am hard-pressed between the two, having a desire to depart and be with Christ, which is far better. (Phil 1:21–23)

Overcoming Barriers to Evangelization in Japan

> Now if Christ is preached that he has been raised from the dead, how do some among you say that there is no resurrection of the dead? But if there is no resurrection of the dead, then Christ is not risen. And if Christ is not risen, then our preaching is empty and your faith is also empty. (1 Cor 15:12–14)

These are topics that can be discussed while traveling on a train, visiting a coffee shop, or walking about in the neighborhood. For churches, may I suggest holding three informal get-togethers with Buddhist friends annually? These are the meetings to which members are encouraged to bring their neighbors to come.

The first one is to be held around Easter. It is a splendid time to talk about his resurrection. Let your Buddhist friends voice their doubts and listen to them carefully. Give the laypeople a chance to explain their own beliefs. It will have a salutary effect of leading them to cast away their own doubts. Use this as a time of establishing a point of contact with the Buddhist community that hopefully will last, thus creating evangelizing opportunities.

In that spirit you could then organize a second meeting around *O-bon* when people's attentions are pivoted toward thoughts of their ancestors. Your guests will be asked a question: "Where do you think your departed ones are today?" Listen to their answers carefully. More likely than not, their answers will be "in paradise." But many of them will not be sure. It is at this point that you can speak about the certainty of his redemption.

The third meeting should be held around Reformation Sunday. The Japanese people have insatiable appetite for Western history. Explain how the Reformation came about, and do not forget to mention the abuse of indulgence.

In Buddhist funerals, one of the rituals would involve the giving of a posthumous Buddhist name called *kaimyo*. Originally *kaimyo* meant the name given to a person who has taken the vow of the Three Treasures. Gradually there developed a notion that even after death, one could become a Buddhist by receiving a posthumous Buddhist name from a priest. That name was supposed to assure a better life in the next transmigration. Then several ranks

Barrier II: Buddhism Enmeshed in Japanese Culture

were created. The higher the rank, the better it would be to assure salvation for the departed. Choosing the lowest rank? No one would dare think of doing that.

The rank and required amount of donation are subject to negotiation. The grieving party always loses the bout. The fee for the highest rank is exorbitant. It is an important source of income for the temples, and its abuse is rampant. They are selling salvation for money just as the Roman church did with indulgence. When your Buddhist friends are exposed to these facts, they may want to take a fresh look at our Reformed doctrine of salvation. That is what we hope to accomplish through these meetings.

In sponsoring these meetings, please make it certain that the format remains informal. Chairs must be arranged to make it easier to engage in conversation. These are not sessions for sermons. Encourage your guests to speak out freely. That is easier said than done in Japan. People are reticent, and do not want to stand out in the crowd. Ask your members to make their guests feel at home. Make members of the congregation your co-workers in Christ, and ask for their full participation. Encourage mixed couples to bring their nonbelieving spouses. That is one of the ways to make your informal gathering (*zadankai*) a success. Doing this you will come one step closer to bringing your Buddhist friends to Christ.

WHAT CAN WE LEARN FROM BUDDHISM?

As we end our discussion of Buddhism in Japan, let us spend a moment reflecting. Why do the Japanese people consider this alien religion called Buddhism their very own, while Christianity remains alien to them? What are the things they do so well that we fall short at? Please consider a couple of things.

First, to become a Buddhist, all a seeker has to do is to say: "I follow Buddha, I follow his teachings, and I follow his monastic order." It is simple and clear. Can we have something similar?

We do have our classes for those who desire to be baptized. It is a good thing to have. But in these courses we often try to spoon feed our basic doctrine without giving seekers time to think on their own. For a grown man to be treated like a child is rather humiliating. As ministers, you may not be aware of that. Zen masters solved that problem through the process of *koan* and *zazen*. When their seekers reach their enlightenment, i.e. *satori*, they are encouraged to express that experience in their own words. We all can learn from this. Instead of giving lectures and recitations of catechism, why not allow participants in the baptismal class to share their conversion experiences in short pithy sentences that everyone can remember. For Luther it was "The just shall live by faith," and for someone in your class it might be, "I surrender all."

On the matter of contextualization, we have a great deal to learn from Buddhism. They have learned to speak the language of the common people and created Buddhist parables and morality tales which have become part and parcel of Japan's folklore. Why can't we do the same? We have a far better message, but by transmitting that message only through the western thought process, we have allowed ourselves to become isolated from the majority of the Japanese people. Our Christian doctrine is one of the greatest accomplishments of Western civilization. Under the influence of Hellenism, and powered by the Aristotelian logic, our systematic theology, in its brilliance, has no peer in any other religious literature. I am not saying that we should avoid transmitting it. But to use it for evangelization is very much like taking a graduate school textbook to be read to the passersby in the middle of a large city. It has nothing to do with their daily lives and will evoke no interest. Jesus taught the meaning of his kingdom by using parables. If early Christianity had not developed in the Roman world under Hellenism, but rather took roots to the East traveling through the Silk Road and beyond, it certainly would have taken a different shape and expression. It is time for us to help our Christian brothers to find ways to express our Christian thoughts and values in the Japanese language more consistent with their daily lives.

Chapter 3

Barrier III
Myriad Deities of Shintoism

> When I go away to the sea
> I may become a corpse under water
> When I go away to the mountain
> I may become a corpse in the grass
> It is for my emperor that I shall die
> Regret I have absolutely none.[1]

THIS 1937 DITTY, SET to the tune by Nobutoki Kiyoshi (1887–1965), was sung more frequently than Japan's national anthem during the Second World War. Tens of thousands of Japanese soldiers and sailors were sent to their death in the Pacific theater with this song. The original stanza came from a long poem of the Manyo poet Otomo no Yakamochi (718–785), who also left an oft-quoted phrase "indeed my emperor is my god." Ancient Shintoism

---

1. My translation. "*Umi Yukaba*" was one of the theme songs in the movie *Tora, Tora, Tora*, a collaborative film with American and Japanese actors depicting the events that led to Japan's attack on Pearl Harbor, December 7, 1941.

Overcoming Barriers to Evangelization in Japan

had its origin in the ancestor worship practices of great clans. It was a means through which they could gain their clan solidarity. Once the imperial clan succeeded in having its deity recognized as supreme above all others, it used emperor worship to solidify its control over the entire nation. In the eighteenth century, these old Shinto beliefs were resurrected in the form of national studies to create a coherent anti-Bakufu ideology. It was adopted by disenchanted samurai to bring about the Meiji Imperial Restoration of 1868.

Like Buddhism, Shintoism claimed that it possessed a mythical power to protect the nation. And like Buddhism, it received generous support from the state and prospered. In 1868, the Meiji government decreed that Shintoism and Buddhism should be separated, and covertly sanctioned the destruction of Buddhist statues and temples. Behind these decisions was an attempt to revive the practice of emperor worship. At a time when the government did not have sufficient resources to quell rebellions, it became a cheap substitute for an army that was yet to be built. When Emperor Meiji died, he was enshrined in the Meiji Shrine. In 1895, the Heian Shrine was dedicated, commemorating the 1,200-year anniversary of Kyoto becoming the capital of the nation. Its deity was Emperor Kammu, the emperor who moved the capital to Kyoto. In both of these instances there was an attempt to strengthen the practice of emperor worship.

The cult of emperor worship was dormant during the Taisho period (1912–26) while Japan experimented with western-style parliamentary democracy. But the onset of the worldwide depression changed it all. Nationalism and militarism were revived, and with it came the practice of fervent emperor worship that again deified the emperor.

This came to a screeching halt with Japan's defeat in the Second World War. Japan was put under US occupation, whose main goal was the demilitarization of Japan. Among the policies adopted by the occupation authorities was to forbid state subsidy for Shintoism. On New Year's Day, 1946, Emperor Showa declared:

Barrier III: Myriad Deities of Shintoism

> The ties between Us and Our people have always stood upon mutual trust and affection. They do not depend upon mere legends and myths. They are not predicated on the false conception that the Emperor is divine, and that the Japanese people are superior to other races and fated to rule the world.[2]

This rescript effectively ended the myths that as the direct descendent of the Sun goddess, the emperor was a living god. This had been the cornerstone of state Shinto beliefs.

After Japan regained her independence in 1952, there were attempts by some former ultranationalists to reestablish emperor divinity myths, but these efforts never took hold. Today the state does not subsidize Shintoism, and all shrines have to operate as religious associations.

There is an organization called the Association of Shinto Shrines that overseas about 80,000 shrines and regards the Grand Shrine of Ise as the one providing the foundation for their belief. Ise is where the Sun goddess, Amaterasu Omikami is enshrined, and currently Emperor Akihito's daughter serves as its high priestess. In this you may detect that there is an undercurrent of a desire to reestablish ties between the imperial household and Shintoism. These ties do exist. When a new emperor ascends to the throne, its ceremony follows closely the rituals set by the ancient Shinto practices.

I apologize for not giving an overview of Shintoism, as this has never been the intent of this book. What I am hoping to do here is to point out a few sensitive issues that may be raised when you approach Shinto believers. It is for this reason the above topic is discussed first. Here are a few other issues we must also consider.

Can Christians Visit Shinto Shrines? Yes, you can visit almost any shrine. Meiji Shrine, for example, can be considered a historical

---

2. www.ndl.go.jp/constitution/e/shiryo/03/056shoshi.html, page 1, reproduces the text of the Imperial Rescript Denying His Divinity, published in Kanpo Gogai Showa Niju-ichi Nen Ichi Gatsu Tsuitachi (Official Gazette, Extra, January 1, 1946).

site. It contains a museum dedicated to Meiji history, and is worth a visit. The Heian Shrine's Japanese garden is one of the must-see sites in Kyoto. Don't hesitate visiting these shrines. Your visit does not constitute an act of worship. If any of your Japanese Christian friends question you, you can cite the above-mentioned Emperor Showa's denial of divinity declaration that there is really no god enshrined there.

Things become complicated when Yasukuni Shrine is involved. Established in 1869, it is the shrine dedicated to the memory of those who died in service of Japan. On the surface it shares the same sentiment we express toward our Arlington National Cemetery. It is a right thing to do to honor those who died in service of their country. The problem with Yasukuni, however, is in its insistence that those who died for Japan must be worshiped as gods. It lists 2,466,532 names as deities, including 1,068 who were convicted of war crimes during the Pacific war. Yasukuni became the center of controversy when it was found that the list also included the names of fourteen A-Class war criminals.

Yasukuni has spring (April 21–23) and autumn (October 17–20) festivals. In war-time Japan, these were the dates that the emperor came in person to worship at the shrine. In recent years, visits, or "worship," by a sitting prime minister have become quite a hot political issue. I hope you will pay close attention whenever this issue is raised. It provides an excellent opportunity to discuss who our God is.

Life-affirming Aspects of Shintoism and its Festivals: Close ties with militarism in the past casts a dark shadow over Shinto, but we must not overlook the fact that there is a positive life-affirming side to Shintoism. If you have been in Japan long enough, you will have seen one of the many festivals held in Shinto shrines. If, for example, you are in Kyoto in the month of July, you will invariably encounter the assembling and procession of Gion Festival floats. While the floats are assembled, the town folks beat drums, sing songs, and dance in the street to support the endeavor. Once

Barrier III: Myriad Deities of Shintoism

the procession starts, the entire city becomes engrossed in the festivities. The shouting in unison of the young people pulling the floats mesmerizes people and transfers their youthful energy to the entire town.

Or you may go to any shrine on the 7-5-3 children's festival. Happy faces are everywhere, full of joy, with abiding faith and hope for the good things to come in the future. Festivals have been the sustaining force for Shintoism. They have also served the function of cementing community solidarity. To modern minds, Shinto deities are mere mythical figures, and I doubt many Japanese will consider seriously that these deities have power over their own destiny. Yet according to the *2018 Annual Report of Religious Population*, 47.6 percent of the Japanese consider themselves Shinto believers.[3] This figure is about the same as that for Buddhism and shows Shintoism's continued public acceptance. It is these festivals that have effectively bound the Japanese public to Shintoism. Shared memories of their youths and a sense of belonging to one's own community, or what the Germans call *gemutelichkeit*, are all present in these festivals.

As a missionary, if there is a festival in town, I hope you will become one of the onlookers. Take your children along with you, and make your presence known. As you make yourself a familiar figure to them, your chance of reaching them will increase dramatically. If you feel uncomfortable going to these "pagan" festivals, please read 1 Corinthians 8 for guidance.

A Calendar of Shinto Festivals: Let us now take a quick look at some important Shinto festivals. .

New Year's Day: Shrines perform ceremonies to expel evil spirits, and pray for a good harvest of the five grains for the year.

Setsubun: A holiday to celebrate the end of winter on February 3 or 4. It is accompanied by a bean-scattering ceremony to expel evil spirits.

---

3. *2018 Annual Report of Religious Population*, www.bunka.go.jp/tokei_hakusho.../pdf/h30nenkan_gaiyo.pdf, 3.

Spring Equinox Day (March 20 or 21): Celebration of the official change of seasons. Shrines offer prayers for the healthy growth of the five grains.

Day of Cleansing (*Ooharai*; June 30 and December 31): A ceremony is performed to expel evil spirits and prayers are offered for good health. Most Shinto families do their semi-annual house cleaning on this day.

Autumn Equinox Day (September 22 or 23): To celebrate the change of seasons. Visit to ancestral graves during this week (*Ohigan*).

First Crop Festival (*Kannamesai*; October 15–17): Offering of the first crop to the deities.

Festival for Seven-Five-Three (*Shichi-go-san*; November 15): This is one of the most delightful Shinto festivals. It is a rite of passage for girls aged three and seven years old, and boys aged three and five years old.

Labor Thanksgiving Day (November 23): This is a national holiday which has its origin in Shinto's *Niinamesai*, thanking the deities for the year's abundant harvest.

Off With Coal Dust Day (*Susuharai*; December 13): A day to give a thorough cleaning to the entire house so it can welcome the deities for the coming year.

Please keep in mind that this list is far from complete. To make it complete you must add to your list festivals sponsored by local shrines. For each season, they usually have festivals going on for the community. Ask your Japanese friends to make a list for your area. It will come in handy when you want to make contact with Shinto believers.

Incidentally, the local deity is usually referred to as *ujigami*. The term is a carryover from ancient times when each group believed that a particular *kami* was both their ancestor and their protector. Parishioners are called *ujiko*, or children of the clan (*uji*). The relationship that *ujiko* have with the community is called *musubi*, a tie that binds them in harmony from generation to generation.

Barrier III: Myriad Deities of Shintoism

Contextualizing Tips: The above list shows Shintoism's close ties to Japan's agrarian past. Here is a question for you to ponder: Can this religion answer the needs of urbanized Japanese people today?

At the same time, let us not forget that both the Old and New Testaments contain many wonderful stories about agricultural practices of the people of Israel.[4] The parable of the sower found in the three Synoptic gospels (Matt 13:1–23, Mark 4:1–20, and Luke 8:4–15) can easily find its parallel stories in Japan's folklore. Ask your Japanese colleagues to find these stories for you, and use them in your conversations with Shinto believers.

They may come back to tell you that they did just fine without any help from our God. Your response should show his common grace: "He makes his sun rise on the evil and on the good, and sends rain on the just and on the unjust" (Matt 5:45). God did not punish Japanese people for their unbelief, as Shinto deities would, but nurtured them. He, not the myriad deities, has made the sun to shine and the rain to fall so Japan will have abundant crops. God loves Japan, and its people have always been in his plan of salvation.

What is Shintoism? Unlike Christianity and Buddhism, Shintoism does not have basic sacred scriptures. There was an attempt to make the *Kojiki* (*Records of Ancient Matters*), compiled in 712, its scripture, but it gained no wide acceptance. This book, incidentally, contains myths about the creation of the Japanese islands, struggles between the imperial and Izumo clans, the subjugation of the latter, and the births of many deities.[5]

The word Shinto comes from two *kanji*, 神道, the first letter, *kami*, can be loosely translated as "spirits" and the second, the "way." It is a belief system that follows the way of the spirits.

---

4. *Young's Analytical Concordance to the Bible* (Thomas Nelson, 1982), 920, lists for the word "sow" fifty-four entries from the old testament, and forty-four from the new testament.

5. An authoritative translation can be found in Donald L. Phillipi, tr. *Kojiki* (Tokyo: Tokyo University Press, 1969).

Overcoming Barriers to Evangelization in Japan

Kami is present everywhere and is close to human beings. The force of nature itself is also *kami*. The spirits of typhoons, cyclones, volcanoes, earthquakes, huge trees, or anything that is awe-inspiring are worshiped as *kami*. Any awe-inspiring animal can become *kami* as well.

People who had distinguished themselves in their lifetime are often enshrined as *kami* to be worshiped. *Kami* is not always good or benevolent. People who had wreaked havoc on the community may also be worshiped as *kami* so they would cease their malevolence.

How many *kami* are there? Shintoism's answer is contained in the word *yahoyorozunokami*. When translated into English, this word can mean "eight million" or "infinite."

Here is what Motoori Norinaga (1730–1801), a major figure in the Shinto revival movement, said about *kami*. "I do not yet understand the meaning of the word '*kami*.'"[6] He went on to list all the homonyms in *kanji*. Their meanings varied, such as "spirit," "paper," "upper," "hair," "adding beauty," "adding taste," and so on. As a classicist, he thought all spiritual beings of heaven and earth that appear in the classics should be worshipped. He then gave his approval to all spirits that are worshiped in local shrines.

Shintoism does not have a set day for worship. An act of worship can be performed by entering through a *torii* (gateway) to the Shinto precinct, going to the ablution basin to wash hands and rinse one's mouth, and then on to the *haiden* (place of worship). There the visitor bows down twice, claps his hands twice, and then bows down once again to complete the worship. In clapping, as the two palms are placed together, the visitor must lower his right palm about an inch below the left. After clapping twice, the right palm is raised one inch to meet the left. In this the left represents the spirit, and the right the visitor. This same act of worship can

---

6. See Ookubo Noriko, "*Motoori Norinaga no Kami no Teigi ni tsuite* (On Motoori Norinaga's Definition of Kami)," in *Journal of the Association of Japanese Intellectual History* ajih.jp/backnumber/pdf/28_02_04.pdf., 132. Her citation comes from Norinaga's *Kojikiden* (*Exegesis on Records of Ancient Matters*) Vol. 3.

Barrier III: Myriad Deities of Shintoism

be performed at home before a *kamidana*, a miniature household altar.

Purification is the most important ritual in Shintoism. In public, it is done with the priest's wand, but one can purify on his own with water by washing, rinsing, and bathing. Purification rites were performed in the olden days to ward off pestilence. People were encouraged to bathe as a matter of religious purification. That is one of Shintoism's legacies to Japanese civilization as shown in their love for bathing in *onsen*, or hot spring spas, today.

God and *Kami*: From Dr. James C. Hepburn on down, I have the greatest admiration for those people who have translated the Bible into Japanese and brought Christianity to Japan. But I have a bone to pick with all of them. Why couldn't they have found a better word to translate the word God than the word *kami*? As shown above, even the most respected Japanese Shinto scholar could not find an apt word to describe what *kami* really is. *Kami* is a word that is suitable for a polytheistic religion, but it is not suitable for the transcendental and only true God of ours. In contrast, early translations to Chinese avoided the same word entirely. "In the beginning God created the heavens and the earth." The Protestant version used the word *shang-di* (上帝), or "Lord of hosts," and the Catholic version used the term *tian-zu* (天主), or "Lord of heavens," to avoid the pitfall that the word *kami* represented.

Recently I had a long phone conversation with a close friend of mine. We had gone through middle and high school together in a very selective educational program. Highly respected in his profession, he is well read in Western literature and philosophy. As both of us are advanced in age, we freely talked about death. Citing Paul, I said to him that to die in Christ is gain, because there is that promise of eternal life. His reply was totally unexpected. "When I die, I can see that I will merge with eternity. But that is not to say that I will be with your god. To me, whenever I read the Bible, the word *kami* always conjures up the myriad gods of Shinto." I cannot find a better man than he who practices Christian virtues the way

Overcoming Barriers to Evangelization in Japan

the Bible teaches.[7] Yet the mistranslated word about God has so far prevented him from accepting Christ with his whole heart.

It is of utmost importance when we speak to our Japanese friends about God that a clear distinction is made that our God is not the *kami* of Shintoism.

You can always cite chapters and verses to tell our friends about our God. Here is a statement by the theologian Charles Hodge (1797–1878) which summarizes our views very well:

> The Scriptures declare God to be just what we are led to think. He is when we ascribe to him the perfection of our own nature in an infinite degree. We are self-conscious, so is God. We are spirits, so is he. We are voluntary agents, so is God. We have a moral nature, miserably defaced indeed, God has moral excellence in infinite perfection. We are persons, so is God. All this the Scriptures declare to be true. The great primal revelation of God is as the "I am," the personal God. All the names and titles given to him are revelations of what he truly is. He is the Elohim, the Mighty One, the Holy One, the Omnipresent Spirit; he is the creator, the preserver, the governor of all things. He is our Father. He is the hearer of prayer; the giver of all good. He feeds the young ravens. He clothes the flowers of the field. He is Love. He so loved the world as to give his only begotten Son, that whosoever believeth on him might not perish but have everlasting life. He is merciful, long-suffering, and abundant in goodness and truth. He is present help in every time of need; a refuge, a high tower, an exceeding great reward.[8]

---

7. Dr. Tsuji Moriaki (1928–2019) was a brilliant student throughout his life. After graduating from Tokyo University's Medical School, he remained there as a research assistant and was slated to be appointed to its faculty when his father suddenly died. Without hesitation, he left this prestigious post and returned to his hometown of Kofu to become a plain country doctor, inheriting the family practice in existence since 1773. Following the family tradition, he and his wife Setsuko cared for the sick and assisted the indigent. From the latter they never asked for any payment. This family's saga is told in Tsuji Kunio's fictionalized *Icho Chiriyamazu* (*Leaves from Ginkgo Tree*). This footnote is added after his death, but with his prior permission.

8. Charles Hodge, *Systematic Theology*, vol. 1 (New York: Scribner, 1873),

Barrier III: Myriad Deities of Shintoism

Putting on my Japan specialist hat, I would like to encourage you to visit as many temples and shrines as possible to gain Buddhists and Shintoists for Christ. However, there is a cautionary note. Some shrines exhibit phallic symbols as deities to be worshiped. That reminds me too much of Ba'al. Sometimes it will be good to read out loud to them the first part of the Ten Commandments:

> You shall have no other gods before Me. You shall not make for yourself a carved image—any likeness of anything that is in heaven above, or that is in the earth beneath, or that is in the water under the earth; you shall not bow down to them nor serve them. For I, the Lord your God, am a jealous God, visiting the iniquity of the fathers upon the children to the third and fourth generations of those who hate me, but showing mercy to thousands, to those who love me and keep my commandments." (Exod 20:2–6)

Approaching Followers of Shintoism: Surfing the internet to examine the current state of Shintoism studies, I discovered an intriguing fact that Shintoism scholars are interested in studying the Bible so they might be able to create a system of theology akin to what we have. This initiative comes from professors at Kokugakuin University, which is the premier institution that trains Shinto priests. If so, this opens up a golden opportunity for us to spread the good news to this segment of the Japanese population.[9]

Can I suggest that you create Bible study groups that will attract these Shintoism followers? In this you will need the help of your Japanese congregation and friends. If you already have Bible study groups in existence, you can utilize them, but the more the

---

9. Kokugakuin has exhibited in its museum early versions of the Bible translated into Japanese through the Taisho period ending in 1926. They offer a course based on the English Bible and another one on the Revelation. See the following sites: museum.kokugakuin.ac.jp/event/. . ./2017_japanese_translation.html, syllabus.kokugakuin.ac.jp/view.aspx?year=2017&regno=3447, and https://www.kokugakuin.ac.jp.

merrier. Try to create a number of small groups, each not exceeding five members. Each of these groups can meet to determine the book they want to study, and try out how well they can proceed with what they have selected. Once that is accomplished, members can jointly invite two or three neighbors who are Shinto followers to join them. Meetings should be held at the homes of Christian members on a rotating basis, and not in church or at the missionary's home. This is to give the participants a sense of being at home and with their own people. At each of these meetings, the host should serve as the chair of that meeting.

I can guarantee that each of these meetings will be a success with your participation. You can add spice to their Bible study by giving the same lessons in English, perhaps after they have studied those same passages in Japanese among themselves.

Can small groups like these do much for evangelization? Major accomplishments in history often came from small beginnings. Jesus had only twelve disciples. Apple got started in Steve Jobs's bedroom and then garage. Shoka Sonjuku was the school that trained a significant number of leaders of the Meiji Restoration of 1868. It was started in an eight-*tatami* room. Shintoists' interest in the Bible gives us a unique opening. Let us take full advantage of it.

Other Ministry Tips: Your ministry to Shinto believers can start with a simple question. "Who is your god?" Or, more precisely, "Who are your gods?" Unless you are in a rural area among old people, you are not likely to get an answer. There may be very few city folks who have *kamidana* (Shinto altar) at home and know the names of their deities, but they are in the distinct minority. They may attend public Shinto ceremonies where priests will read blessings in the language of ages past. It is something like a mass offered in Latin that no one can understand.

Your next question should be: "What do you believe?" In your travel across Japan you will find folks who suddenly stop in front of a mighty tree or a rock and start bowing and clapping. They are Shintoists. Why do they do it? They have encountered

Barrier III: Myriad Deities of Shintoism

spirits residing in these trees and rocks and want to be on the safe side with these spirits. They want to propitiate the anger of these spirits so they do not become objects of their retribution (*tatari*).

If you have been in Japan long enough, you know what the word *tatari* means. Ask your Shinto friends what that word means to them. *Tatari* can fall upon a man unawares, and the anger of gods is totally unpredictable. This conversation can lead you to a discussion about sin, which is an act of man's willful disobedience to God and alienation from him. The concept of sin is totally absent in Shintoism. You know the rest. You now have an opening to discuss the act of redemption through the precious blood of Christ.

You should not challenge their belief system directly. The apostle Paul shows us how to reach them:

> I perceive that in all things you are very religious; for as I was passing through and considering the objects of your worship, I even found an altar with this inscription 'to the unknown god.' Therefore, the One whom you worship without knowing, him I proclaim to you: God, who made the world and everything in it, since he is Lord of heaven and earth, does not dwell in temples made with hands. Nor is he worshiped with men's hands, as though he needed anything, since he gives to all life breath, and all things. (Acts 17:22–25)

Ghost Stories: Ghosts often appear alongside myriad Shinto deities. In his *Ghosts of the Tsunami*[10], Richard Parry relates his experience of hearing about ghost sightings across the Tohoku region after the 2011 disaster:

> After the tumult of the disaster has settled down a bit and everyone has enough to eat, has shelter, and has their minimum resources, that's when people finally start to

---

10. Richard Lloyd Parry, *Ghosts of the Tsunami: Death and Life in Japan's Disaster Zone* (London: Jonathan Cape, 2017). Parry is the Asia Editor and Tokyo Bureau Chief of *The Times* (UK), and has lived in Tokyo for the past 22 years.

reflect on the whole experience. That's when trauma and PTSD[11] start to manifest themselves—and also when the ghosts begin to appear.[12]

Parry of course does not believe in ghosts, but observes that: "for those people who encounter the supernatural, the experiences are very real. They're symbols of the massive trauma that the Tohoku region and the whole culture of Japan experienced." This is an issue we must ponder seriously. What should the Christian message be? During his interviews, Parry met a Buddhist priest who performed exorcisms. Then there was a Christian minister who quietly served the needs of people possessed by the spirits of the dead.

Learning from Shintoism to Lead Them: As we get to know Shintoists and learn from them, they will in turn show us a way to reach them. Roger Lowther is an American missionary in Tokyo who loves Sumo, Japan's national sport which was started around AD 700 as a way to amuse Shinto deities. He found in it a lesson for Christians, and also a way to reach his Japanese friends. Here are Roger's words from his "Wrestling for a Blessing":

> Every year, professional sumo wrestlers visit my children's kindergarten and beat *mochi*, a kind of rice cake. They pick up really large heavy wooden mallets and pound the rice over and over again until it becomes a thick solid cake. Usually at some point during the day, the kids will be allowed to jump and hang on to the sumo wrestler. It's quite a picture! A huge man will have thirteen or so children hanging from him! The only way a strong man like this can interact with the children is to hold back his strength. . .is to hold back his weight. He needs to make doubly sure that he does not accidentally step or lean on any of those children."[13]

11. Post-Traumatic Stress Disorder.

12. Parry's interview held at International House of Japan, Tokyo. "How a British Journalist Sees Japan." *I-House Quarterly* 18 (Summer 2018) 8–9.

13. Roger W. Lowther, "The Broken Leaf: 50 Meditations on Art, Life,

Barrier III: Myriad Deities of Shintoism

This reminded him of the biblical story of Jacob wrestling with God. Roger could not figure out this passage: "You have struggled with God and with humans and have overcome" (Gen 32:28). He then came to this conclusion:

> The only possible way Jacob could have won is that God held back his strength. The only way God could say, "You have wrestled with God and have overcome," is that God deliberately made himself weak—so weak, in fact, that he could not even overpower Jacob. And through the weakness of God, Jacob was victorious. Like the sumo wrestlers with the children, God must have held back his strength and held back his weight as he wrestled with Jacob. Jacob could only meet God in his weakness, because God's strength would kill him.
>
> So, here is the only way that this story makes any sense. It all points to Jesus. Jesus is the greater Jacob. Jesus is the wrestler to whom the story points. Jesus' defeat in weakness is our triumph, and through Christ's loss we have victory.[14]

This is a beautiful exegesis, and one sure to please his Japanese audience. What Paul teaches in 1 Corinthians 9:20–22 comes down to this: "If we want to bring more Japanese to Christ, we must become more like Japanese." Roger has done so, and in the Sumo parlance, he has entered their *dohyo* (the ring inside which the wrestlers compete) successfully. May I urge you also to enter that ring, the *dohyo*? From there you will be able to observe Japan from within!

SOME REFLECTION

When you go to Japan, and need a place to meet someone, a Shinto shrine is always an attractive candidate. The Shinto precinct is easily accessible and is a friendly place to visit. Everyone can enter

---

and Culture in Japan" (Unpublished manuscript, 2018), 245–51. Cited with author's permission.

14. Lowther, "Broken Leaf," 251.

its gate. Without having any regular worship services, Shintoism still has been able to maintain close ties (*musubi*) with its *ujiko* (parishioners) due to this openness. It claims that all residents of the local community are its *ujiko*, and everyone is welcomed to its festivals. Do our churches have this sense of close ties with the local communities? Why do our Japanese friends continue to have a perception that churches are only for their believers and that their doors are closed to others? "Come to me, all you who labor and are heavy laden, and I will give you rest" (Matt 11:28). This sweet and powerful invitation of our Lord is for all who seek him. Missional churches must find ways to open their gates.

Chapter 4

Barrier IV
Seeking Perfection Without God

"WHAT IS THE CHIEF end of man?" we ask. We have our answer in the *Westminster Shorter Catechism*, but let us consider this question being asked of Japan's general public. Individually, you may find different answers. But as a group, they will likely point out to you the following objectives of education as providing an image of the perfect and most desirable person.

These objectives of education are contained in the second article of Japan's 2006 Basic Act on Education as follows:[1]

(1) Having students acquire wide-ranging knowledge and culture, fostering the value of seeking the truth, and cultivating a rich sensibility and sense of morality as well as building the health of the body;

(2) Developing individuals' abilities, cultivating creativity, and fostering a spirit of autonomy and independence . . . .

(3) Fostering the values of respect for justice, responsibility, equality between men and women, and mutual respect and

---

1. "Basic Act on Education," www.mext.go.jp/en/policy/education/lawandplan/title01/detail01/1373798.htm.

cooperation, as well as the value of actively participating in building our society and contributing to its development, in the public spirit;

(4) Fostering the values of respecting life, caring about nature, and desiring to contribute to the preservation of the environment; and

(5) Fostering the value of respect for tradition and culture and love of the country and regions that have nurtured us, as well as the value of respect for other countries and the desire to contribute to world peace and the development of the international community.

The 2006 Basic Act on Education was a complete revision of the 1947 law which was promulgated under the US occupation. Under the new law, efforts were made to restore old Japanese values. Some have even argued that next to amending the constitution, changing the education law was the most important thing that could be done. Every process of education is tightly controlled centrally by the Ministry of Education, Culture, Sports, Science and Technology. It is this ministry that administers this law, and the above-cited objectives represent the public's consensus views.

"Acquire wide ranging knowledge and culture... to contribute to world peace," says the law (see objectives number one and five). It is a good image of man. Behind it is the humanistic tradition that man can achieve perfection through his own effort. The measure of man is man, and nothing more. Greek philosophers taught this to us, and Japan has been deeply influenced by it since the Meiji Restoration of 1868.

Confucianism in Japanese Tradition: The idea that man can perfect himself by his own bootstraps was not unknown to the Japanese before the coming of the West. Confucianism, which came to Japan centuries earlier, taught exactly the same message to generations of Japanese. Confucius's basic teachings can be summarized in one word *ren* (仁, in Japanese *jin*), which can

Barrier IV: Seeking Perfection Without God

variously be translated into English words like "benevolence," "love," "goodness," or "humanity." It is the supreme virtue. Thus:

> The resolute scholar and the humane person will under no circumstances seek life at the expense of humanity. On occasion they will sacrifice their lives to preserve their humanity.²

Confucius loved learning: "Having heard the Way (*Tao*) in the morning, one may die content in the evening."³ He also spoke about his own journey to perfection:

> At fifteen, I set my heart on learning. At thirty, I was firmly established. At forty, I had no more doubts. At fifty, I knew the will of heaven. At sixty, I was ready to listen to it. At seventy, I could follow my heart's desire without transgressing what was right.⁴

Confucius's goal in life was to create a society in perfect harmony with the will of heaven. It is a society where children are filial toward their parents, and people yield to each other by the principle of reciprocity. "Do not do to others what you would not want others to do to you."⁵

Confucianism came to Japan in the sixth century. However, it did not spread widely until the Tokugawa period (1603–1868). The prolonged peace established under the Tokugawa rule turned the samurai class into civil servants who had to lay down their swords for books. Study was encouraged by all levels of the government. In 1630, the Bakufu granted a piece of land to Hayashi Razan (1583–1657) to establish a center for Confucian learning. In 1790, it became in effect Japan's first university directly administered by the government. In the Tokugawa administrative structure, the next level was called *han*. It was a domain governed by a *daimyo* (a holder of a large fief). Most *han* also established their own schools.

---

2. William Theodore de Bary, *Sources of Chinese Tradition* (New York: Columbia University Press, 1960), 29. Reprinted with permission of the publisher.

3. de Bary, *Sources of Chinese Tradition*, 25.

4. de Bary, *Sources of Chinese Tradition*, 24.

5. de Bary, *Sources of Chinese Tradition*, 27.

Their basic texts were the four books and five classics of Confucianism. As for doctrine, they all adhered to the neo-Confucian philosophy of Zhu Xi (1130–1200). His moral philosophy can be summarized as follows: Man's fundamental nature is good, and his mind is in essence with the mind of the universe. One can become perfect and overcome his own limitations by studying the underlying principles in the universe. Zhu Xi called this process the investigation of things. The things to be investigated are not material things, but matters of personal conduct, human relations, and political affairs. Individuals are encouraged to become scholars to attain *ren* (or *jin*, "humanity"). The road to perfection lies in self-cultivation.

During the Tokugawa period, education spread to common men, merchants, townfolk, and rural villagers. Most temples set up schools to teach children how to read, write, and count. The basic text for these temple schools (*terakoya*) was the Japanized version of the *Three Character Classics* (*sanjikyo*) which contained basic teachings of Confucianism along with *kanji* needed for daily living. Education spread so widely in Taokugawa Japan that in the middle of the nineteenth century, Japan became perhaps the most literate nation in the world. Sociologist R. P. Dore estimates that "by the time of the Restoration (1868) forty to fifty percent of all Japanese boys and perhaps fifteen percent of girls were getting some formal education outside their homes."[6]

This Confucian legacy was maintained by the new imperial government through the end of the Second World War. Education became compulsory through the sixth grade. In grade schools and middle schools, all students were required to take a course called *Shushin*, meaning "self-cultivation." This ethics course was firmly based on Confucian precepts. *Shunshin* is no longer taught in Japanese schools. After the war, the American occupation authorities abolished it because it had also been used as a means of promoting emperor worship. Yet its Confucian roots had a salutary and

---

6. R. P. Dore, "The Legacy of Tokugawa Education," in Marius B. Jansen, *Changing Japanese Attitudes toward Modernization* (Princeton: Princeton University Press, 1965), 100.

Barrier IV: Seeking Perfection Without God

long-lasting effect on Japanese society. They have encouraged solidarity among neighbors, as well as sacrificing self for the good of the community. *Shushin* may be gone, but Confucian teachings have survived. The behavior pattern that emerged in the seventeenth century has been reinforced generation after generation without interruption.

On March 11, 2011, Northeast Japan was devastated by a magnitude 9 earthquake, which was followed by a tsunami and a nuclear disaster, resulting in the death and injury of 24,590 persons.[7] It was the worst natural disaster in Japan's post-war history. The world witnessed a sight seldom seen elsewhere. In spite of their own suffering, losing loved ones and properties, victims of the disaster yielded to one another. On the television screen, all could be seen was the rectitude, self-sacrifice, and a willingness to help others. It was remarkable because the ones helping others were in desperate need of help themselves. It was a triumph of will and to borrow Churchill's words, their "finest hour." All of that was nurtured by centuries of Confucian teachings.

These characteristics of Japanese people I have just described make them the most desirable candidates to receive the word of God. Their actions are exemplary, and their hearts are in the right place, seeking to do good for others. At the same time, their goodness becomes a huge stumbling block. They would argue that they can attain perfection without knowing our God. This is the conundrum we have to face and which requires some elaboration.

Perfectibility of Man: Humanism in Greece and its variation under Confucianism have contributed significantly to world civilization. However, behind the declaration that man can become perfect with his own effort, is a notion that the existence of God is not essential to man's existence. In spite of its avowed liberalism, humanism has an exclusionary element. Those who disagree with their basic premises are deemed unlikely to attain perfection. During the

---

7. Wikipedia, "Tohoku Earth Quake and Tsunami" (Japanese version), https://ja.wikipedia.org/wiki/東北大震災.

Tokugawa period, a number of Confucian scholars termed Japan "the true Confucian gentleman's land in East Asia," differentiating Japan from China—where Japan received Confucianism from in the first place. It was an attempt to put down those who disagreed with their exegesis of Confucian texts, but more importantly to express their national hubris. This national hubris is what we have to counter. It could reject Christianity in this fashion: "We have such and such wonderful virtues in our hands. So, we really don't need your God."

"Man is the measure of man" is what humanism espouses. With that yardstick, if someone says "God is dead," he has not committed any offense. However, if someone does not follow politically correct rules, he may be sued and lose his job. Unfortunately humanism cannot set the moral standards that can apply equally and fairly in every situation. In today's society, the higher the perceived power of humanism becomes, the greater the chance that society will create more reasons to reject Christianity. Earlier in this book I dealt with the barriers presented by Buddhism and Shintoism, but the greatest barrier may be found in the attitude of self-reliance nurtured by Confucianism because it has given the Japanese people a sense of general satisfaction with their own tradition.

How to Reach Out: What is the best way to reach out to these good people? Let us begin by taking a look at Japan's education system. We must give a lot of credit to its success. It has produced world-class scientists and scholars, including a significant number of Nobel Laureates. It has effectively answered society's needs for educated manpower, and the nation is the most literate, standing shoulder to shoulder with other most advanced countries.

Yet problems abound. There is a phenomenon called examination hell that forces middle and high school students to study for entrance examinations to the next levels of schooling. Schools are ranked not by the quality of its education, but by the number of students they can place on the acceptance lists of best universities.

Barrier IV: Seeking Perfection Without God

It is estimated that 10 percent of high schools do not teach what they are supposed to teach and are content to let their students prepare for university entrance exams.[8] Parents spend a fortune to send their children to a place called *juku*, a tutoring establishment whose sole purpose is to prepare children for entrance examination. Examination hell has claimed its toll, as evidenced by high levels of teen suicides. Another factor in the teen suicides is bullying, which the Japanese call *ijime*, an issue that has never been adequately addressed by the authorities. There is also the issue of rigidity of school curricula. The education bureaucracy, highly centralized in Tokyo, is itself the problem and cannot provide answers.

Japan, like the United States, does not allow religious education to be part of its public education. It is up to our Christian community to redress this issue on our own, and here are some steps for you to consider.

Religious Education at Home: Education must begin at home. "And you fathers, do not provoke your children to wrath, but bring them up in the training and admonition of the Lord" (Eph 6:4). Christian education is not just to teach the Bible, but also to teach by the example parents set before their children:

> You shall lay up these words of mine in your heart and in your soul, and bind them as a sign on your hand, and they shall be as frontlets between your eyes. You shall teach them to your children, speaking of them when you sit in your house, when you walk by the way, when you lie down, and when you rise up. (Deut 11:18–19)

Whatever one has taught his children in their youth, it will stay through the rest of their lives, and will even go beyond their generation as Proverbs 22:6 attests. "Train up a child in the way he should go. And when he is old he will not depart from it." It is

---

8. See Dorothee Franz, "The Revised Fundamental Law of Education and Japan's Bid for Educational Reform."

Overcoming Barriers to Evangelization in Japan

echoed by Joel 1:3: "Tell your children about it. Let your children tell their children, and their children another generation."

When can the education start? It can begin immediately after the birth of a child, and even before while the child is still in his mother's womb. The Japanese language has a beautiful word for it, *taikyo*, combining two *kanji* characters, "womb" and "teaching."

How can you, as a foreign missionary, become part of this education process which you advocate for your Japanese friends? It is simple. Please visit their homes and answer their needs. Your presence will have a great impact on the children's young lives.

May I share with you my childhood experience? I grew up in Keelung, a port city north of Taipei, when Taiwan was still Japan's colony. Many missionaries from overseas and Japan stopped by our home before they went on to their destinations. My memories of them are vivid. Whenever a missionary arrived by boat, he was met by our young assistant minister, who would bring the missionary to our home to rest. Those were exciting times for me and my older brother. My brother, six years older than I at age 96, has in his lifetime amassed a collection of materials concerning missionaries in Taiwan which he has donated to Tainan Theological College. He maintains a well-visited website for the study of Christianity in Taiwan.[9] As for me, I used to encourage my students who had missionary parents or grandparents to write papers about their missionary activities in lieu of mid-term exams. The fact that I am writing this book, which is dedicated to your work as missionaries to Japan, cannot be dissociated from my early encounter with missionaries. I was only eight or nine years old when the assistant minister taught me a few phrases in English, and with that I greeted two Canadian missionaries. Their smiles I can still visualize today. That constituted one of the fondest memories of my childhood. Sorry to write about me, but the point I want to make is clear: your visit to these Christian homes will be remembered for a long time by the children.

In Japan, a house visit usually calls for an *omiyage*, a little something to present to the hostess. Please do not let this deter

---

9. http://www.laijohn.com.

Barrier IV: Seeking Perfection Without God

you. Instead of spending money to buy a box of candy, why not consider creating something that can be useful for children's education? Write down lessons in English and print that out for children. You can also enlist the help of your Sunday school classes to create things that can appeal to different age groups. Let your imagination be your guide.[10]

Creating *Juku* in the Fashion of Home Schooling: In the United States, many parents have opted for home schooling to avoid the secular anti-Christian education prevalent in public schools. My local church has an effective system of supporting home schoolers by sponsoring luncheon meetings and sports events for them. The church also holds ceremonies for them when a new academic year starts, and when they graduate. In this way, home schoolers will never feel isolated. Using this as a model, I would like to encourage our Japanese Christian friends to actively consider creating a home-school style *juku* for their children.

Juku's sole purpose is to train students to become adept in taking entrance exams for the next level of schooling, and its tuition is exorbitant. The education it provides is not true education, but a technique to read quickly and answer quickly so one can pass the test. What I am proposing here is to provide an alternative. Today's parents are well educated. They can consult among themselves to find the courses they can comfortably teach. They can pull their resources together to conduct a *juku* in their own homes on a rotating basis. Let us call it a home-*juku*. Parents will study the subjects together with their children, teaching them not techniques, but substances, and imparting to them the joy of learning. If this is successful, invite non-Christian neighbors to join in. They can add some Bible lessons in between to make the home-*juku* into a means of evangelization. It is almost like killing not two, but

---

10. Also consider writing a thank-you note after your visit. It will be very much appreciated by the host family and will make them feel closer to you. Children especially will love it. Success in evangelization often comes from a sense of affinity developed through little things like this.

three birds with one stone: saving money, teaching kids to succeed, and evangelizing nonbelieving neighbors.

Churches can hold regular meetings for these home-*juku* people, like their American counterparts do for their home schoolers. You as missionaries can add spice to these meetings by teaching English from the Bible. Those who go to established *juku* will look upon it with envious eyes.

Bible Times: I am sure you have had experiences in teaching English from the Bible. However, at times you may wonder how to sustain it over a long period of time. Here is how one mission team has solved that problem successfully.

Open House Conversation School is an outreach program of MTW's mission team in Chiba. It has a program called "Bible Times," which is a thirty-minute, free add-on to the one hour of English conversation. Then after having coffee or tea together, the group would open the Bible and follow a text with well-placed questions and answers to continue their conversation. You can access their Bible time texts at https://esol4j.wordpress.com/. Written mostly by its former head teacher, Linda Karner, over a period of twenty years, these texts are time tested. They will become quite useful if you want to maintain a long-lasting program.

Properly administered, "Bible Times" can become a very effective means of reaching the unchurched and strengthening the faith of those who are already with us. Its informal setting as part of a conversation school is a big plus. Repetition is part of the game, and fine points of the doctrine can be driven to the minds of those who are attending. The normally reticent Japanese people feel freer to ask questions. There is flexibility in choosing topics and lengths of time.

Linda's TESOL (Teaching English Abroad) module, "Story of Jesus in Luke," ran nine trimesters for three years. This format allowed her to ask several key questions. For example, while studying Luke 9:23, "If anyone desires to come after me, let him deny himself, and take up his cross daily, and follow me," she asked her

Barrier IV: Seeking Perfection Without God

students "Does 'deny yourself' mean saying 'yes' or saying 'no?'" and "Is it easy to say 'no' to yourself?" Pointing out how difficult it is, sometimes, to say "no" to even one cookie, she gives this admonition:

> To follow Jesus there are other times to say "no." For example, many Japanese people, many of you, go to the Shrine and the Buddhist temple. You are used to worshiping there. This is your custom. It is your culture. But if you follow Jesus, you have to say "no" to Buddhism and Shintoism. That would be very difficult! That would be the killing of a part of yourself—like dying on a cross. I think this is what Jesus means.[11]

The beauty of this passage is it has allowed Linda to contextualize her message and warn new believers not to backslide into old Shintoist and Buddhist practices. Strange as it may seem, this stand taken by Linda will receive support from Confucians and humanists who, as iconoclasts, cannot contradict her, while in all other matters they may still disagree with her. Contextualization in a variegated cultural tradition is a complex and challenging business. The flexibility inherent in "Bible Times" will allow you to find and experiment with new approaches.

Here I have spoken about flexibility. Linda has another series based on Handel's *Messiah*. She explains:

> This thirteen week Bible time series was developed to accompany a CD of selections of Handel's *Messiah*; the CD was then our Christmas gift to the students that year. Using Handel's *Messiah* gave us the opportunity to look at some difficult passages with our students, as well as the many passages showing God's tenderness and love.[12]

---

11. Hard Things, The Story of Jesus in Luke, Part 4, 2011 Open House Bible Times, cited with permission from the author. https://esol4j.files.wordpress.com/2011/03/02-follow-christ.pdf, 3. Scroll down to the fourth segment, click 02 Follow Christ. Second paragraph on second page.

12. https://esol4j.wordpress.com/2007/11/11/handels-messiah-teachers-notes/. Scroll down close to the end, and stop at Handel's Messiah—Teacher's Notes for the text of the quoted passage.

Overcoming Barriers to Evangelization in Japan

Linda teaches regularly in a Christian school.[13] In the fall of 2017, one of her students came to visit me with her. He read the Bible for me in Greek and Hebrew. It was a remarkable feat. In a school that held the word front and center in its curriculum, his urge to know the Bible in its original languages became insatiable. He, of course, did not need any help in English conversation, but others did through "Bible Times." Mingling with them, he found his own talent and calling. Economists would call this a multiplier effect. One blessing leads to another blessing. It is worth it for you to consider adopting "Bible Times" for its multiplier effect in your ministry.

Teaching Bible as Literature: When you have a chance, I hope you will encourage your mission board to train and recruit people who can teach Bible as literature and then be placed in Japan's many private schools.

English has not been taught well in Japanese schools, and a good teacher of English is hard to come by. The inability to speak foreign languages fluently is considered a serious handicap for Japanese businesses. To redress this situation, Kyoto Sangyo University, for example, annually sends off more than 10 percent of its students overseas, and is actively recruiting foreign students to come and reside in its dormitories.[14] There is an urgent need for good English education, and in fact many secondary schools are actively recruiting better English teachers. The suggestion I am making here is to fill this gap and gain a chance to reach the unchurched.

It is not an easy task. Those qualified to teach Bible as literature may not know the Japanese language adequately. To train them requires long-term planning. Short term though, there can be compromise solutions. An American teacher can team up with his Japanese counterpart and jointly conduct a course. If you look around there are many opportunities to do so.

---

13. Covenant Community School International in Chiba.
14. https://www.kyoto-su.ac.jp/.

Barrier IV: Seeking Perfection Without God

In this you should focus on private schools which are less encumbered by government regulations. Private schools also do better academically. One of the best indicators of the best schools is determined by the number of graduates who have successfully passed the entrance examination to Tokyo University. Of the ten best in 2018, eight were private schools.

If your church or denomination is already operating a school in Japan, please actively consider exchanging your teachers with private schools in your area. The relationship you establish will go a long way toward propagating his word to the next generation of Japanese.

What is Family? Have you ever thought about this question seriously? Whenever we speak of our family in the west, we point to our nuclear family. But in Japan, the word conveys an entirely different meaning. It refers to the extended family and to ancestors. Thus, when they say "*uchi wa*" (my family is) to you, you must understand that the full weight of tradition is behind that word. One's action today impacts the family's honor back to previous generations.

Let us assume that there is a young student who wishes to be baptized. One day his grandfather admonishes him: "That is going to displease your ancestors." Just with that much warning, the young man will stop coming to church. If the young man persists, he will be disowned by his family. I have known a number of cases in which my friends chose Christ. "If anyone comes to me and does not hate his own father and mother, wife and children, brothers and sisters, yes, and even his own life, he cannot be my disciple" (Luke 14:26). They had taken these words very seriously. I still remember one friend's expression: "It was almost like getting a death sentence when I was disowned by my family." I hope you know your Japanese co-workers well enough to ask them this question. "Has your family ever threatened to disown you?" Your ministry can start from there.[15]

---

15. Zen Buddhism also had to wrestle with the issue of an individual's

The importance Confucianism places on family, however, gives us an opportunity to discuss our covenant theology. God's covenant with Abraham was not given to him alone: "I will establish my covenant between me and you and your descendants after you in their generations, for an everlasting covenant, to be God to you and your descendants after you" (Gen 17:7). We, who are in Christ, are also Abraham's descendants: "And if you are Christ's, then you are Abraham's seed, and heirs according to the promise" (Gal 3:29). The promise contained in these passages is far greater than any word Confucius could provide.

Contextualizing Christian Messages with Confucianism: Conversations with Confucians will always be a delightful and rewarding experience. Their doctrine is life-affirming and they adhere to high moral standards. Jesuit missionaries who went to China in the seventeenth century even thought of recommending Confucius to be canonized. Thankfully we do not have to worry about that issue. In any event, you will find in your Confucian friends seeds of religion (*semen religionis*) well planted within them. One can find in Confucianism many instances of "a revelation of God, an illumination of the Logos, and an operation of God's Spirit."[16]

There are so many stories in Japanese history, literature, and even in children's literature which are imbued with the Confucian sense of right and wrong. They can be incorporated into a sermon to interpret Christian values. Take for example, the story of Kiuchi

---

satori against his family connection and came upon these words: "If you meet a Buddha kill him. If you meet a patriarch of the law, kill him. If you meet your father and mother, kill them. . ." These words are found in *Rinzairoku* (first published in 1120). Kawabata Yasunari (1899–1972) cites these words in his 1968 Nobel acceptance speech "Japan the Beautiful and Myself." See Lu, *Japan*, 610.

16. These are the words of Dr. Herman Bavinck (1854–1921), the Dutch theologian, as quoted in the fourth paragraph of Homer C. Hoeksema's "Calvin's Theory of "Semen Religionis," (Seed of Religion)" which is a well-written and must-read article on this subject. It is available at: http://commongracedebate.blogspot.com/2016/10/calvins-theory-of-semen-religionis-seed.htm.

Barrier IV: Seeking Perfection Without God

Sogoro (d. 1653), a village headman in the domain of Sakura. Lord Hotta of the domain was corrupt, merciless, and exacted exorbitant taxes on the farmers. Sogoro appealed to every level of the government to reduce the tax burden, but to no avail. The only way left was to appeal to the Shogun directly, but that was punishable by death to his entire family. He went ahead and appealed directly. As he successfully divorced his wife, she was spared of the death penalty, but he was crucified and their three children were beheaded. In spite of it, the substance of his appeal was granted and farmers were relieved from the heavy tax burden imposed by the Hotta family. In 1851, this story was made into a popular Kabuki play. In a Japanese literature class in my high school, our teacher, who was not a Christian, ended his remarks with this biblical quote: "Greater love has no one than this, than to lay down one's life for his friends" (Luke 15:13). He then added that Sogoro did more by sacrificing his own children's lives as well. In Japanese, substituting one's life for another's is called *migawari*.[17] It is a word easily understood by everyone because it expresses well the love behind the act of self-sacrifice. Yet the supreme sacrifice of the Son of God, the Lamb of God, who was led to slaughter for our sins does not register much in the minds of the Japanese. One of the difficulties is found in the word *shokuzai* (贖罪) as a translation of the word "redemption." It is a word found only in the Bible and used only among the Christian circles, thus the concept remains alien to the Japanese public. Referring to the story of Sogoro, and using words like *migawari*, would enable us to bring the concept of redemption much closer to the Japanese people's shared experiences.

---

17. The story I gave here is from one of many different versions. Another version tells us that his wife was also crucified. Mariana Nesbitt, in her *Jesus for Japan: Bridging the Cultural Gap to Christianity* (Kindle, 2017), cites this story as her favorite to start a discussion on how to use Japanese literature as a bridgemaker between Christianity and Japanese culture. She knows Japan. The terms and concepts she explains in her book will be very useful to other missionaries. Incidentally, the Sakura domain was located roughly around the same area occupied today by the Narita Airport. In the city of Narita, there is a temple dedicated in memory of Sogoro.

Overcoming Barriers to Evangelization in Japan

There is a heartwarming story of *migawari* that happened on the snowy night of February 28, 1909, in Hokkaido. A passenger train was climbing up the steep slope of Shiokari Pass when the last carriage was uncoupled. It started sliding backward very quickly. A mid-level railway official was a passenger. He went out to the deck to apply the hand brake. When the sliding became uncontrollable at a bend, Nagano Masao (1880–1909) threw down his own body on the railway track to serve as a brake. The train stopped, and a major disaster was avoided.

Nagano carried his last will and testament in his pocket. The rescued passengers found it on his body. In it was this statement: "I thank God and dedicate everything to him. . . I pray that one day my death may become a catalyst for my brothers and sisters to know God and the true meaning of being thankful to him."[18] Nagano became a Christian a decade before his death. Born in a family of samurai whose forebears served as tutors to the domain's lord, Nagano was raised strictly in the Confucian tradition. His upbringing taught him that Christianity was an evil religion that demeaned Japan's sacred past. Miura Ayako turned the story of Nagano into a highly acclaimed work of fiction called *The Shiokari Pass*.[19] In it, the spiritual struggle of Nagano traveling the two worlds of Confucian and Christian values was well documented. There was also a confluence of the two values that had made Nagano the man that he was. Made into a major motion picture in 1973, it became an important topic of discussion in religious and intellectual circles. There are many more stories like these cited here that can help you reach out to our Japanese friends.

A challenge for missionaries is how to find these wonderful stories. May I suggest that you form a regularly scheduled seminar on contextualization with your Japanese colleagues? Each of you will bring a story to the table and discuss how that story might be

---

18. My translation. Nagano's last will is carved on a monument erected in his honor at the site of his death. Google search "Images for Nagano Masao" for the picture of this monument.

19. Miura Ayako, *Shiokari Toge* (Tokyo: Shincho Bunko, 1969). Bill and Sheila Fearnehough's English translation, *Shiokari Pass*, is available in paperback from OMF (1984).

Barrier IV: Seeking Perfection Without God

used to give gospel messages. This can be done at your retreat as well.

May I also suggest that you make an effort to learn many of Japan's familiar sayings? Your language skill will improve dramatically, and you will become a better conversationalist. You can compare these sayings with those in the wisdom literature of the Old Testament. It will create an opportunity to talk about our God without giving an appearance of overtly doing so. Subtlety always works well in Japan.

Making Your Church into a Cultural Center: Roger Lowther, who graced our pages in the last chapter, is an organist and heads an organization called Community Arts Tokyo. He explains this organization as follows:

> Community Arts Tokyo is dedicated to connecting people through the arts. We are a local community-based group in Tokyo's historic downtown area (*shitamachi*) reconnecting the arts to society and our daily lives. Art helps us to understand the world around us, respond to it, and wrestle with it. It then gives us the vision and power to bring about the future we seek, for the flourishing of humanity at local, national, and global levels.
>
> Community Arts Tokyo offers performances, lectures, symposiums, lessons, masterclasses, screenings, and exhibitions. We are responsible for a wide range of music education, from college preparation for overseas study to children exposed to music for the very first time. We remain closely connected to the professional art world in Japan through formal events (concerts, panel discussions, etc.) and informal events (fellowship dinners, sharing times, parties, etc.). We also work to connect and provide resources for churches from many denominations and groups through the arts and worship.[20]

---

20. www.communityarts.jp/home/, paras. 1-2.

Overcoming Barriers to Evangelization in Japan

Mission to the World (PCA) reports a heartwarming episode about its activities:

> A Japanese woman and her husband recently moved back from England. While there she'd become a Christian... She is a gifted player of the *koto* (Japanese harp) which has always been her status symbol and identity. When she became a Christian, she instead found identity in Christ and considered giving up music completely. A Tokyo church plant hired her to play for the Good Friday service, and she discovered that her skill could be used in praise of God instead of a substitute for God.
>
> Over the following months, MTW's Community Arts Tokyo team involved her in many events that brought her deeper into Christian community... She no longer wants to give up music, but is instead beginning to write Japanese worship songs and become more deeply involved in serving the church through worship.[21]

Art knows no borders, and it is the avenue through which we can reach more Japanese people than through other conventional means. Churches can learn from the example set by Roger. In the earlier chapter on Buddhism, I have suggested that you consider holding tea ceremonies and *ikebana* schools in your church. Here may I add on another to make your church into a cultural center for your community? To do so you must first survey your community to find out what your neighbors need and want. Then consider what your church can provide for them. You may want to invite local choral groups to perform in your church. There may be colleges around you from which you can find hidden talents. Consider incorporating traditional Japanese art forms. We have seen here a success story in *koto*. How about *rakugo*, a monologue talk show that is ingrained in common folks' culture? Dr. Saito Kazuo is a scientist with Hitachi. He performs *rakugo* for church groups with aplomb and brings out clear Christian messages. There are limitless opportunities to utilize Japan's traditional art forms. And when that is done, your Japanese friends will find closer affinity with your church community.

---

21. Letter from Lloyd H. Kim, Coordinator, MTW, dated April 10, 2018.

Barrier IV: Seeking Perfection Without God

It is an adventure to explore unfamiliar venues. Trust in the Lord that he will provide needed tools to accomplish your end. If you cannot find them, you simply have not searched far enough. "Ask, and it will be given to you; seek, and you will find" (Matt 6:6).

While living in Kyoto, I marveled at the ease with which I was able to obtain a ticket for a live performance of Beethoven's Ninth Symphony, because it was performed more frequently in Japan than in any other part of the world. Handel's *Messiah* is equally popular. Amateur choral groups organized to sing *Messiah* can be found in almost every city, including Asuka, Nara, where the first Buddhist temple was built in Japan in the sixth century. Have you ever thought seriously of tapping into this energy and enthusiasm for Christian music exhibited by those seekers who are still unchurched?

Confucius loved music. "When Confucius was in Zi, he heard the Shao music and forgot for three months the taste of meat, saying: 'I never thought music could be so beautiful.'"[22] The Japanese people love music and art. Let us hope your encounter through these venues will result in a good harvest.

REFLECTION

In the preceding three chapters, I have stressed the importance of knowing various aspects of Japanese tradition. Why is it so important to us? Let us ponder the reason why Christ waited until the age of thirty before embarking on his teaching journey. Jesus could have started teaching at age twenty, but he did not. As a youth he was full of wisdom. At age twelve, he sat in the temple in Jerusalem "in the midst of the teachers, both listening to them and asking them questions. And all who heard him were astonished at his understanding and answers" (Luke 2:46–47). In fact at the tender age of twelve, he could have taught. However, Jesus was raised in a Jewish community, and he observed their tradition. He scrupulously followed what was taught in Numbers 4:3: "From

---

22. My translation from *The Analects of Confucius* in the original language.

Overcoming Barriers to Evangelization in Japan

thirty years old and above, even to fifty years old, all who enter the service to do the work in the tabernacle of meeting."

Just as Jesus respected Jewish tradition, we must respect Japanese tradition when we wish to serve him in Japan.

Respecting Japan's tradition can pay rich dividends when approached wisely. Okuno Masatsuna (1823–1910) was a samurai who fought against the Meiji government. He once sought to become a Buddhist priest, and was a Confucian scholar of note. He met J. C. Hepburn in 1872 to assist him in the compilation of the second edition of his Japanese-English dictionary. He also assisted Samuel R. Brown (1810–1880) in his translation of the gospels. The two missionaries sought his help because of Okuno's knowledge of Japanese classics. Okuno was not a Christian, and there was no assurance that he would ever become one.

In 1873, Okuno heard James H. Ballagh (1832–1920) preach on the subject of Peter's denial of Christ. Suddenly he was overwhelmed by the thought that he had known Christ all along, but denied him just like Peter had done thrice. He immediately asked to be baptized. Okuno continued to assist Hepburn's Bible translation and became a minister and hymn writer. He and his Japanese colleagues were able to transform missionaries' words into elegant Japanese prose. They made Psalms, Song of Solomon, and Isaiah into literary gems that would impact modern Japanese literature.

Chapter 8 of Acts gives us a story of an Ethiopian eunuch asking to be baptized by Philip (vv. 24–40). He was a traditionalist who read the Old Testament and went to Jerusalem to worship. It was at a time when Saul and other Jews persecuted Christians, and one could easily surmise that he would be of the same mind. Yet Philip's words changed it all. This passage teaches us how to approach people who are raised in other traditions. It gives us great hope and encouragement. Common grace provides a bridge of understanding, and with prayers and supplication, the Holy Spirit will guide us.

I hope in your missionary work in Japan, you will have a chance to meet your Rev. Okuno.

Chapter 5

Barrier V
Invisible Proscription

IN 1612, THESE WORDS were prominently displayed on the public board (*takafuda*) in Nagasaki: "No one is allowed to become a follower of the padre. Offenders shall be severely punished." A year later all priests were expelled from the country and in 1614, proscription against Christianity became the law for all of Japan.[1]

Today Japan does not proscribe Christianity and its constitution guarantees freedom of religion. However, there are invisible proscriptions, just as the United States has experienced proscriptions through the guise of political correctness. Let us first examine briefly what political correctness has done to America.

"The notion of political correctness came into use among Communists in the 1930s as a semi-humorous reminder that the Party's interest is to be treated as a reality that ranks above reality itself," writes Angelo M. Codevilla, Professor Emeritus of

---

1. Documents relating to the proscription of Christianity and the closing of the country may be found in Okubo Toshiaki et al., *Shiryō ni yoru Nihon no Ayumi (Japanese History through Documents) Kinseihen (Modern Period)* (Tokyo: Kobunkan, 1955), 121–33. See also C. R. B. Boxer, *The Christian Century in Japan, 1549–1650* (Berkeley: University of California Press, 1951), and Lu, *Japan*, 197–201, 220–28.

International Relations at Boston University. "The semi-humorous reminder went something like this: 'Comrade, your statement is factually incorrect.' 'Yes, it is. But it is politically correct.'"[2]

Political correctness is defined by Wikipedia as follows:

> The term political correctness is used to describe language, policies, or measures that are intended to avoid offense or disadvantage to members of particular groups in society. Since the late 1980s, the term has come to refer to avoiding language or behavior that can be seen as excluding, marginalizing, or insulting groups of people considered disadvantaged or discriminated against, especially groups defined by sex or race.[3]

On the surface, it appears that political correctness was for the protection of the minority. But the progressives have turned it into a weapon to obtain cultural hegemony for themselves. The minority could be a racial minority, or a group of homosexuals. It did not matter who they were, as long as their rights were protected. From there it went on to create a myth that saying "Merry Christmas" was injurious to the general welfare of some because it would upset those who were not Christians. The next step was to make gay rights a major political issue, and anyone who did not support it was deemed a bigot who denied civil rights to his fellow countrymen.

Under normal circumstances, political correctness would not have gained much traction. But the new wave of anti-establishment sentiment after the Vietnam War created a fertile ground for a new iconoclastic ideology, and political correctness rode that wave to great success.

The term "cultural hegemony" was popularized by Antonio Gramsci (1891–1937), an Italian Marxist and politician. It envisions a small group of elite ensconced in universities, government,

---

2. Angelo M. Codevilla, "The Historical Origin of 'Political Correctness,'" para. 3. www.intellectualtakeout.org/blog/historical-origin-political-correctness. It was originally published in *Claremont Review of Books*, Nov, 2016

3. Wikipedia, "Political Correctness," para. 1. https://en.wikipedia.org/wiki/Political_correctness.

Barrier V: Invisible Proscription

and media taking charge of a nation's culture, dictating what one can believe and what one cannot. In America, Hollywood has joined this elite group. The threat to their hegemony comes from God, and naturally his influence has to be denied. A speech code has been carefully drafted. Mention of God is objectionable, but mention of Allah is not. To the cultural elite, Christianity and the values it represents can have no place in America's public square.

In 2015, the US Supreme Court, by a five-to-four margin, legalized same-sex marriage. It represented a solid triumph for the left in the ongoing cultural war. The left succeeded in this by relentlessly suing those who opposed their views in lower courts, and by having elite schools accept their speech code.

To Japan's credit, political correctness has not landed on her shores. Perhaps it is due to the fact that the Christian population in Japan is only 1.1 percent, and there is no need for the Japanese left to fight this 1.1 percent. But the Japanese people have their own version of cultural warfare. It comes in the form of secularism and nihilism. To combat this invisible opponent, notable Buddhists even seek Christians out as allies. In 1994, I was the featured speaker for the Kansai Area Buddhist Conference, attended by fifteen heads of major Buddhist sub-sects in the area. I started the meeting by briefing the group about the cultural war staged by the politically correct crowd in America, in the manner similar to what I have described on the first two pages of this chapter. At that point I was interrupted by one of the participants. "Oh we have a similar problem!" It was an informal setting, and for the remaining one hour and a half, we simply exchanged views. If I spoke about the difficulties that Christian schools had to face in America, I would be joined by the chorus of how difficult it had been to operate Buddhist schools in Japan. If I bemoaned the constant attack against our cherished Christian values, they would tell me how difficult it had been for them to protect Buddhist values. The meeting ended with the chair of the group giving this admonition: "Let us hope that Buddhists and Christians will work together to combat the

Overcoming Barriers to Evangelization in Japan

sea of unbelief in this world, or else we may all be swallowed up by them."[4]

In chapter 2, I have described how strongly entrenched Buddhism has been in Japanese society. They have created a barrier for us which has been difficult to overcome. But at the same time, they also face similar invisible enemies and are less prepared than we are. There is a time to join forces with them as well as a time to fight against them.

Lack of a significant overt movement toward political correctness does not mean that Japan is invulnerable, and there are many danger signs. First, the Japanese people are very sensitive to what is taking place in the Western world. Whatever happens in New York, Los Angeles, and Paris can become the rage of the day in Tokyo the next morning. If someone has decided to use political correctness to seek redress for any perceived social ills, it could spread rather quickly. All it takes is a few rabblerousers. Second, the notion of privacy, once absent in the Japanese vocabulary, is now strongly ensconced in the Japanese psyche. Suppose there is a sexual pervert who engages in illicit behavior, but wins his case as a matter of privacy.[5] That could easily happen. Third, like their counterparts in the West, Japan's mass media are left-leaning and are tolerant of new morality. Fourth, the Japanese people consider it a virtue not to poke into other people's business. That was exactly the same attitude the American public had when political correctness was just beginning its nascent march. Their little victories here and there in school boards and local courts were overlooked by the public as nothing significant. But before the public realized what was happening, the politically correct crowd's small victories

---

4. It was a bittersweet event for me, since it was held in honor of my friend and mentor, the late Kiuchi Nobutane, who was vice chair of its national organization, but became a Christian before his death. See chapter 2, pages 28–30.

5. The subculture called *moe* and *otaku* refers to feelings of strong sexual attraction to anime and manga figures. In 2004, Kobayashi Kaoru kidnapped and murdered a seven-year-old. It was widely believed that Kobayashi was a *moe* pervert. Some businesses, well established in Tokyo's Akihabara district, cater to this perversion. They have a strong financial basis to launch a legal challenge to make this perversion into an accepted practice.

Barrier V: Invisible Proscription

became precedents which in turn set restrictions on practicing Christianity as we have known in America since the founding of the country. Let us hope same thing does not happen in Japan.

The danger that the politically correct crowd poses for America is not confined to the visible and invisible barriers they have created against our worship of God, but also in their impact on the thought processes of Generations X and Y. Will these generations succumb to the crowd's godless philosophy and discard the Christian values of their fathers? This same challenge is very much present in today's Japan.

What values do Japanese youths hold dear to their hearts today? Presumably most Japanese are Buddhists, Shintoists, or both, but how many really believe in their Buddha or *kami*? Alienation from traditional religions is often felt most significantly among the youth. The spiritual vacuum thus created has often been filled by new religions like Soka Gakkai and Rissho Koseikai, which are offshoots of Nichiren Buddhism. It is also filled by cults such as Aum Shinrikyo, whose founder and six key members were executed simultaneously in July 2018. It reminded the public afresh of the terrorist sarin attack on Tokyo's subway system in 1995.[6] Those who were executed were once brilliant scientists and a doctor. They could have had successful careers. But spiritual vacuity is an entirely different matter which is difficult to fathom.

The left and the politically correct's pitches are softer and subtler. They do not bark at you. They do not threaten people who do not join them with Armageddon, or engage in murder and mayhem. Instead they inundate the airwaves, television, mass media, and even manga and anime for children to offer worthless entertainment to implant in the youths values that are not normally accepted. Eventually those who accept their new values will reach a critical mass. Their next step is to shame those who do not subscribe to these new values. Shame is a key word here. In olden days, samurai fought to gain honor, and even committed *seppuku* to blot out any shame on their names. Not to conform can be a shameful act. Who can then oppose this new morality in Japan?

6. *Nippon Keizai Shimbun*, July 6, 2018.

Overcoming Barriers to Evangelization in Japan

In this way, the left can win, and their cultural hegemony will become complete. In the process they will create all roadblocks against Christianity (and other belief systems.) These are what I call invisible proscriptions.

Christian Answers to Invisible Proscription: What are the most effective ways of dealing with these invisible proscriptions? The first and clearest answer is to pray for the people who created these proscriptions. "My son, do not despise the chastening of the Lord, nor be discouraged when you are rebuked by him, for whom the Lord loves he chastens, and scourges every son whom he receives" (Heb 12:6). The book of Hebrews was written for Jewish Christians who were exiled and lived in Rome, and many allusions were made to Roman customs. It was the custom of the Roman nobility to subject the heir of the household to a training regimen comparable to slavery, while other sons were allowed to live in luxury. This regimen that had differentiated the heir from other sons was actually a manifestation of the father's love for his heir. Thus we must thank our Lord for giving us these trials for the purpose of making us his true sons. Trials will strengthen our faith. We must thank all those who have brought these trials on us.

Let us stop for a moment to think. Have we really been his good and faithful servants? Japan enjoys freedom of worship, yet the number of Christians remains static at 1.1 percent. In neighboring China, a Christian can be prosecuted. Yet Asia Harvest tells us that 7.7 percent of Chinese are Christians, and the number is growing year after year.[7]

This is not a conundrum and an answer can be found readily. In China, people who believe live out their faith. They do not

---

[7] These figures were obtained from https://asiaharvest.org/how-many-christians-are-in tables-china-/when I first accessed them on July 8, 2018. The detailed statistical tables are no longer posted by Asia Harvest obviously for security reasons. Please consult its latest update in their Newsletter #158, July 2019 https://asiaharvest.org/wp-content/uploads/paper-newsletters/pdf/158-jul-2019.pdf for the closing of churches, disappearances of house church leaders, and use of facial recognition technology to discourage church attendance. Chinese churches need our prayers.

Barrier V: Invisible Proscription

know if they will be arrested the next day. There is seriousness in their belief, and they are eager to impart the good news to their neighbors. That is how, in spite of the watchful eyes of the Chinese government, Christianity has spread across the nation there. When a Christian is placed in safe surroundings, his faith may be only skin deep, and his words will lack credulity. Peter and Paul both experienced imprisonment. Peter died on a cross, hanged upside down. Paul was beheaded. "For to me, to live is Christ, and to die is gain" (Phil 1:21). The apostles wrote their letters while their lives were hanging in the balance. Readers of their letters, in spite of persecution, read them eagerly. This was how early Christianity gained traction. When we have forces who try to oppress us, those who create visible and invisible barriers against us, we must pray for them, and thank our Lord for training us to become better servants of his.

The second step you must take is to take a serious look at your Bible, and read it as if you are one of those who are persecuted. Its words will jump at you with meanings which you have not experienced before. Once you have that experience, share that with members of your own family and friends. Then go on to share that with strangers. That is how people in China are bringing others to Christ. If they can do it, why can't we?

The third step will involve your community. Please try to consider how your church can contribute to your community:

> But know this, that in the last days perilous times will come: For men will be lovers of themselves, lovers of money, boasters, proud, blasphemers, disobedient to parents, unthankful, unholy, unloving, unforgiving, slanderers, without self-control, brutal, despisers of good, traitors, headstrong, haughty, lovers of pleasure rather than lovers of God, having a form of godliness but denying its power. (2 Tim 3:1–4)

These were words written by Paul to Timothy, but the conditions he describes are eerily similar to those found in today's Japan. Those who seek help do not get help. There is no place to go and there is no one to talk to. Life is one of painful loneliness. When one gets sick, he goes to a doctor. When he is hungry he goes to a restaurant, when his car breaks down he goes to a neighborhood garage, but when his heart is broken, where can he go? My suggestion for your church is to create a counseling center for your community.

Timothy Keller, in his seminal work *Center Church*, emphasizes the importance of churches to "own their neighborhood," and advises that church leaders "should go to local community boards and neighborhood associations, as well as contact local government officials and representatives to discover how they can best serve the needs of the neighborhood."[8]

Creating a counseling center, in Japanese *soodansho*, will do just that and more. We want to own our neighborhood. In this case, though, instead of church leaders visiting government offices and local boards, we invite people to come to us whenever they need help. The entire church will put their heads together to create and operate it. It is an organization for which everyone will serve as volunteers.

Creating a Counseling Center: Here, the size of your church becomes an important determining factor. There will be differing approaches. The following steps provide a simple guide which must be adjusted to your local conditions:

1. As a matter of principle, this organization is to be manned by church members who serve as volunteers. Ministers may or may not be directly involved.

2. As long as volunteers are adults, no restriction is placed on age. Whether old, middle-aged, or youth, all age groups should be represented.

3. Whether lawyers, government workers, teachers, students, merchants, doctors, nurses, or house wives, many occupations can be represented, and the more the merrier.

---

8. Timothy Keller, *Center Church: Doing Balanced, Gospel-Centered Ministry in Your City* (Grand Rapids: Zondervan, 2012), 176.

Barrier V: Invisible Proscription

4. What will be asked of each volunteer is that he be a sincere Christian, and be willing to spend two hours each week on a regular basis to serve as an advisor.

5. The church office will assemble office hours for these volunteers, create a schedule, and publish it not only in the church bulletin, but also in other means that can reach the wider local community.

6. When matters of church doctrine are raised in counseling sessions and volunteers cannot answer, ministers must be contacted.

7. Volunteers shall conduct a get-together meeting each month to exchange information to help one another. They must always be mindful of respecting the privacy of people they conferred with while exchanging information.

8. As for serving tea and other mundane matters, the church shall set a uniform policy so as not to inconvenience volunteers.

Today's Japanese people face many difficult issues. The population is aging and there are fewer babies born. Who is going to take care of a widowed parent? A list of difficulties and social ills can go on and on: discord among a husband and a wife; mid-life crises; single parasite (an adult, unmarried child living with his parents without performing any household duties); failing an entrance examination; losing a girlfriend or boyfriend; losing a job; contemplating abortion; contemplating suicide; bullying; pornography; the opioid crisis, and so on. These are problems that individuals cannot solve on their own. Or there may be someone who lives alone in his four-and-one-half-*tatami*-room apartment and desperately needs to hear another person's voice. Your job is to create an oasis in this urban jungle to heal the wounds of these lonely and helpless souls.

Jesus taught us to love our neighbors. You must listen to those who come to you carefully, compassionately, and give them encouragement from Christian perspectives. You cannot do this job alone as a minister or a missionary. Enlist the help of your congregation and tap into the resources you find in them. As described above, church members represent many professions and have various areas of expertise. Let them use their expertise to help your neighbors.

The center may not bring a visible benefit to your church immediately, but it will strengthen the faith of those who volunteer. One day, some of those who have come by for advice may decide to attend your Sunday services. Establishing a counseling center is a way to find these lost sheep. The Lord will bless you abundantly.

Writing this far, an image of a former student of mine at his graduation emerged so vividly in my mind. Two and a half years before that date, at little past five, there was a meek knock on my door. That student sat down and spoke with me until past six. I do not remember what he said that day.

At the graduation his eyes shone brightly. "Thank you Dr. Lu for that day," he smiled. "You may not know, I was thinking of committing suicide. I went to several professors, but no one was there. I knocked on your door. If it did not open, that would be the sign that I should go ahead. But then your door opened..." From that day on he took several of my courses, came to my office regularly and visited me at home, but he never told me his secret until his graduation. Without knowing it, God had given me a chance to save a human life. I hope you will seriously consider setting up a counseling center.

Individuals vs. Political Correctness: So far, I have been talking about the church as an organization and how it can solve problems. However, God has also empowered individuals to serve him effectively. As a minister or missionary, please give a message of empowerment to your congregation.

An individual can always be a witness for Christ at home, at his workplace, and as a neighbor. He can always be a good listener and advisor. In Japan, unlike his American counterpart who is under siege by the PC crowd, he enjoys the following advantages:

Barrier V: Invisible Proscription

1. Even though the ratio of Japanese Christians toward the Japanese population is a meager 1.1%, their impact in academia and mass media is far greater than its small number indicates.[9]

2. The ratio of Christians among Japan's leadership class is also significantly higher than its population. Throughout the pre-war and post-war periods, sixty-two persons have occupied the post of prime minister. Of the sixty-two, eight are Christians, or 13 percent.

3. There are close to 500,000 graduates from the so-called mission schools across Japan each year. They have a basic knowledge of what Christianity is all about.[10]

These are favorable conditions. There is a residue of goodwill toward Christian opinion. We need not bow down to the left's false altars. God has given each of us a different talent. Let us use that talent for his glory. Unlike in the past, we no longer need to write a letter to a newspaper or a magazine to express our opinion. Facebook, Instagram, Twitter and many other convenient tools are within reach of every person. An answer you give to a worried youth in puberty can solve his urgent problems. A well-thought-through Christian message can fill someone else's spiritual void.

Have confidence in reaching out to others. The teachings of Christianity are life-affirming messages that contain wisdom

---

9. The other side of the coin is the prevalence of so-called "progressive intellectuals" who dominate Japan's mass media. They maintain that one cannot be an intellectual unless he is a progressive, a refrain familiar to the politically correct crowd in the West.

10. This figure is given in Professor Shimada Hiromi's thought-provoking article "Reasons Why Christianity Did Not Spread in Japan" (*Kirisutokyo ga Nihon de Hiromanakatta Riyu*) in the special winter 2016 issue of *Bungeishunjyu*. The majority of these graduates are women who, once married, would follow their husbands' family tradition with regard to marriage ceremonies and funeral rites. The author maintains that was the major factor in these young women no longer following Christian teachings. I have also dealt with these issues in chapters 2 and 3. However, there is a bright side to this picture. The families into which these mission school graduates married should become good targets for evangelists and church planters to reach.

concerning how to live. When you are able to show this to young people, they will realize that the fads of this world, as well as what the politically correct crowd espouses, are in vain. To lead the next generation to Christ is an important responsibility not just for parents, but for all Christians to share. As individuals we must share that burden with the visible church to which we belong.

What is church to you? When I think about it, memories of my Sunday school years always come into sharp focus. I may think of church as the one I am attending now, its ministers and my many friends in the congregation. My imagination then takes me back to Jesus' time on this earth: the street corner in Nazareth where Jesus played as a little child; Jesus as a carpenter with Joseph; the twelve disciples walking with Christ; and the 5,000 men by the Sea of Galilee. My favorite passage about church comes from Luke 24:13–16.

> Now behold two of them were travelling that same day to a village called Emmaus, which was seven miles from Jerusalem. And they talked together of all these things which happened. So it was, while they conversed and reasoned, that Jesus himself drew near and went with them. But their eyes were restrained, so that they did not know him.

Church is not a building. Church is where Christ is. He is always with us, but oftentimes, like these two disciples on the way to Emmaus, we fail to feel his presence.

To overcome the five barriers we have discussed, let us pray that we will be able to find his presence in our hearts every day. If we all learn how to walk with him, solutions to problems will come naturally to all of us.

Chapter 6

Solution I
Walking With Christ

Our responsibility is to lead others to Christ, and it is important for us to be able to tell them what our beliefs are. How can we explain our basic beliefs in simple and understandable terms? In Reformed circles, we speak of five *solas*. They will allow us to create a portrait of what a man ought to be under God. Let us begin from there.

Sola is a Latin word meaning "only" or "alone," and we have five of them. We follow only the Bible (*sola scriptura*) to know God, only through faith (*sola fide*) can we be saved, we know that only through the grace of God (*sola gratia*) that salvation is given to us sinners, redemption can come only through Christ's death on the cross (*solus Christus*), and man's chief aim in life is to praise his glory only (*soli Deo gloria*). Let us discuss these one by one.

Bible Only (*Sola Scriptura*): How can we know God? It is only through the word of God contained in the Old and New Testaments that we can know him. Peter testifies that "prophesy never came by the will of man, but holy men of God spoke as they were moved by the Holy Spirit" (2 Pet 1:21), and that everything God requires of us on this earth "that pertains to life and godliness" is given to us in Scripture (2 Pet 1:3).

The *Westminster Confession of Faith* elaborates on this point further:

> The whole counsel of God, concerning all things necessary for his own glory, man's salvation, faith, and life, is either expressly set down in scripture, or by good and necessary consequence may be deduced from scripture: unto which nothing at any time is to be added, whether by new revelations of the Spirit, or traditions of men.[1]

This Reformed doctrine set us apart from the practices of the Catholic Church during the Middle Ages that insisted on papal bulls and the church council having equal authority to Scripture. In those days they denied common men access to the Bible. Misuse of papal authority created the sale of indulgence that became one of the main causes of Reformation.

In advocating *sola scriptura*, Luther did not deny other secondary authorities within the church, such as creeds and confessions, as long as they were subordinate to the supreme authority of the Bible. *Sola scriptura* pertains only to man's spiritual being and does not deny the validity of DNA or other scientific discoveries. Knowing the Bible is the key to knowing God. Luther extolled the virtue of a simple layman armed with Scripture as being superior to the mightiest pope or any potentate without it.

This sentiment is echoed in the *Westminster Confession of Faith*:

> All things in Scripture are not alike plain in themselves, nor alike clear unto all: yet those things which are necessary to be known, believed, and observed for salvation, are so clearly propounded, and opened in some place of Scripture or other, that not only the learned, but the unlearned, in a due use of the ordinary means, may attain unto a sufficient understanding of them.[2]

---

1. *Westminster Confession of Faith*, ch. 1, 6.
2. *Westminster Confession of Faith*, ch. 1, 7.

Solution I: Walking With Christ

Luther spoke of the universal priesthood of men. This means that in church planting, laypeople are empowered by *sola scriptura* to work alongside pastors as equal partners.

Through Faith Alone (*Sola Fide*): We can find a summary of Paul's letter to the Romans in the following two verses: "For I am not ashamed of the gospel of Christ, for it is the power of God to salvation for everyone who believes, for the Jew first and also for Greek. For in it the righteousness of God is revealed from faith to faith: as it is written 'The just shall live by faith'"(Rom 1:16–17).

Salvation was very difficult to come by under the mediaeval church. Perfect obedience to God was required of all believers. They also insisted that all believers had to obey the church and the pope, because outside of the church there was no salvation. God's grace that would lead to salvation was dispensed by the church through communion. It had to be taken throughout one's life. As to whether one had been justified in the eyes of God, one had to wait until after death on the day of his judgment.

The young Augustinian monk Martin Luther was a mediaeval man educated in that Catholic tradition. Self-torture and penance and all that was required of him he tried, yet his god was angry, distant, and out of his reach. The notion that "the just shall live by faith" opened the gate of heaven for him. It was a moment of truth that gave him his born-again experience. Man through faith would be reconciled to God and bask in his love and grace forever. Through faith, Luther was able to clearly see God's plan of salvation.

It has been 500 years since Luther posted his ninety-five theses on a Wittenberg church door. *Sola fide* has been one of our basic credos ever since. When our non-Christian Japanese friends find faith in Christ, I am sure they will experience the same joy Luther discovered five centuries earlier. Let us pray for that day to come.

Overcoming Barriers to Evangelization in Japan

By Grace Alone (*Sola Gratia*):

> But now the righteousness of God apart from the law is revealed, being witnessed by the Law and the Prophets, even the righteousness of God through faith in Jesus Christ, to all and all who believe. For there is no difference, for all have sinned and fall short of the glory of God, being justified freely by his grace, through the redemption that is in Christ Jesus." (Rom 3:21–24)

We have learned that we will be justified through faith and it will lead us to salvation. That salvation will come to us only through the grace of God. All of us are sinful creatures ever since-Adam's unpardonable original sin. All of us have disobeyed God and sinned against him. The wages of sin is death. Paul teaches us further:

> And you he made alive, who were dead in trespass and sins, in which you once walked according to the course of this world, according to the prince of the power of the air, the spirit who now works in the sons of disobedience, among whom also we once conducted ourselves in the lusts of our flesh, fulfilling the desires of the flesh and of the mind, and were by nature children of wrath, just as the others. (Eph 2:1–4)

In earlier chapters, we saw Japanese people seeking perfection without God and seeking help from myriad deities. Are they not the same prince of the power of the air that Paul is talking about? The spiritual decay Paul has written about fits today's Japan perfectly. That said, his assurance of God's great love in the following passages should apply equally to Japan.

Paul has also said:

> But God, who is rich in mercy, because of his great love with which he loved us, even when we were dead in trespasses, made us alive together with Christ (by grace you have been saved), and raised us up together, and made us to sit together in the heavenly places in Christ Jesus, that in the ages to come he might show the exceeding riches of his grace in his kindness toward us in Christ Jesus. For

Solution I: Walking With Christ

by grace you have been saved through faith, and not of yourselves; it is the gift of God, not of works, lest anyone should boast. (Eph 2:5–9)

The Catholic church also places importance on grace. The only difference that separates us from them is in the former's insistence that good works have to accompany grace.

John Newton (1725–1807), the hymn writer, went to sea when young, was captured and sold to slavery, and after his rescue he became a slave trader, but gained faith when he was rescued from a sinking ship and then became a pastor. Later in life he became an ardent abolitionist. "Amazing Grace," the hymn he wrote, was, in essence, an autobiography that described his countless trespasses and the abounding grace of God that relieved him from snares of sin. Amazing grace indeed, and that sound is very sweet.

In Christ Alone (*Solus Christus*): John Newton, who was once a slave, was redeemed. Redemption is the word meaning "to buy out." Slaves obtained their freedom after they were bought out and redeemed. We who were enslaved by our sins have obtained our freedom by the blood of Christ, which was shed on the cross. That is all it takes and nothing more. *Solus Christus* is central to our beliefs. We have been "justified freely by his grace through the redemption that is in Christ Jesus" (Rom 3:24). Calvin rejected penance, extreme unction, and ecclesiastical orders as false sacraments, saying that they were not necessary for justification.[3] To depend on these false sacraments or to depend on our own good works goes counter to the doctrine of *Solus Christus*. The *Westminster Confession of Faith* explains:

> We cannot by our best works merit pardon of sin, or eternal life at the hand of God, by reason of the great disproportion that is between them and the glory to come; and the infinite distance that is between us and God,

---

3. John Calvin, *Institutes of the Christian Religion*, tr. by John Allen. 7th American edition (Philadelphia: Presbyterian Board of Christian Education, 1936), 2:746–66.

> whom, by them, we can neither profit, nor satisfy for the debt of our former sins, but when we have done all we can, we have done but our duty, and are unprofitable servants: and because, as they are good, they proceed from his Spirit; and as they are wrought by us, they are defiled, and mixed with so much weakness and imperfection, that they cannot endure the severity of God's judgment.[4]

This is one of the most challenging issues you will ever face in Japan. If you can convey successfully the meaning of *solus Christus* to your friends, you will be able to win them for Christ. At the age of 90, I have had many occasions of sharing the love of Christ with my friends. They will listen to me politely, but more often than not they will simply dismiss my talk as a fairy tale from the Neverland. It is inconceivable for them to think that there is a God so loving that he will send his only begotten Son to die on the cross for us. They may have come from Buddhist families who have been taught that salvation can come only through *nangyo kugyou* (難行苦行), an act of penance going through this life with all sorts of hardships just to obtain merits for the next lives to come. Then that act has to be repeated again and again in the next stages of transmigration. Or they may have come from Shinto families with a leaning toward *Shugendo* (修験道), which also requires a similar act of penance to mortify the passions and the flesh. Jesus dying for ours sins is simply too good to be true for them. With this in mind please study the next two passages with your friends:

> He has delivered us from the power of darkness and conveyed us into the kingdom of the Son of his love, in whom we have redemption through his blood, the forgiveness of sins. (Col 1:13–14)

> For he made him who knew no sin to be sin for us, that we might become the righteousness of God in him. (2 Cor 5:21)

In reading these two passages, it will be good to take an imaginary trip to old Jerusalem with your friends. There is a street

---

4. *Westminster Confession of Faith*, ch. 16, 5.

Solution I: Walking With Christ

named Via Delarosa. We see pilgrims bearing a heavy cross to go up this hilly street. Through this act of devotion they are trying to remember our savior who once walked up this street to his death on the cross. The fact of sinless Jesus bearing our sins to convey us to the glory of his kingdom will become a reality etched in our minds. This imaginary trip is also a good way to share with your friends God's plan of salvation. God knew from the very beginning that we will disobey him and commit all sorts of trespasses against him. But he already had a plan to send Jesus for our rescue, to wipe away all our sins. It is an expression of his unfathomable love. No Buddha or Shinto deity can ever replicate that.

Paul has outlined it very clearly for us in the fifth chapter of Romans. Through one man—Adam—"sin entered the world, and death through sin" (v. 12). And, "for by one man's disobedience many were made sinners, so also by one Man's obedience many will be made righteous" (v. 19). And we all are given the promise of "eternal life through Jesus Christ our Lord" (v. 21). Bear in mind that the last words of Christ on the cross were "It is finished" (John 19:30). At that moment God's plan of salvation was completed. The cross was a symbol of triumph, and there is eternal life awaiting all of us who believe in him. That is the meaning of *solus Christus*.

Glory to God Alone *(Soli Deo Gloria)*: Our heavenly father has given us so much and has showered us with his abundant love throughout our lives. "What is the chief end of man?" asks the *Westminster Shorter Catechism*. Its answer is: "Man's chief end is to glorify God, and to enjoy him forever." For all we have received from him, God asks very little of us in return. It is difficult to fathom the depth of his love for us.

All of us, however, as parents, have this shared experience. When we give Christmas presents to our children, they will say "Thank you, Mom. Thank you, Dad." If they like the gifts we nod in satisfaction. We do not ask much more than that. We do not ask anything in return. We hope our children will be endowed with good Christian values throughout their lives and contribute

Overcoming Barriers to Evangelization in Japan

to society. In Japan this sentiment is often expressed in a simple term: "Do not dishonor the family name." When our heavenly father asks us to glorify him, he is also saying to us "Do not dishonor my name."

As it is written: "Holy, holy, holy is the Lord of hosts; the whole earth is full of his glory" (Isa 6:3). When we glorify God, our every action must follow his will. To be holy is to be away from corruption, immorality, profanity, and depravity.

Psalm 19 starts with these glorious stanzas:

> The heavens declare the glory of God; and the firmament shows his handiwork. Day unto day utters speech, and night unto night reveals knowledge. (Ps 19:1–2)

The concluding stanzas show how God's children must act:

> Who can understand his errors? Cleanse me from secret faults; Keep back Your servants also from presumptuous sins; Let them have no dominion over me. Then I shall be blameless, and I shall be innocent of great transgression. Let the word of my mouth and the meditation of my heart be acceptable in Your sight, O Lord my strength and my Redeemer." (Ps 19:12–14)

This is the way we must act, if we wish to "glorify God, and to enjoy him forever." In so doing, we will be in his presence and so experience "fullness of joy; at your right hand are pleasures forevermore" (Ps 16:11).

Chapter 7

Solution II
Learning from Business Practices

THE PROPHET ISAIAH TEACHES us: "Enlarge the place of your tent, and let them stretch out the curtains of your dwellings" (54:2).

In this chapter, we will discuss church planting. As a missionary partnering with a local church you may not always know what the congregants are thinking. This chapter gives suggestions on how to organize successful teams for church planting and implementing. It is seen from the perspectives of Japanese churches from within. Please beware that they can be quite different from the perspectives you have acquired at home. Please follow these suggestions, step by step, and consult with your Japanese partners. Let them know your concerns candidly, and at the same time do not forget to listen to them carefully and learn from them.

A church is a manmade organization and, as such, shares vulnerabilities with other manmade organizations. When businesses fail, one or more of the following factors are in play:

1. The purpose of the business and its strategies are unclear.

    Have you ever heard of employees complaining? "I don't know why I have to do this?" or "Is there any merit in what I am doing?"

Overcoming Barriers to Evangelization in Japan

That business is sure to fail, because its purpose and strategies are unclear.

2. Poor internal communication.

"What is he doing? Why does he do this?" Starting with simple questions like these, a business can become embroiled in a tug-of-war between different sections or divisions. One section may do something harmful to another section without knowing it. Poor internal communication is the culprit.

3. Prevalence of three M's.

We are not talking about M&M candies. Japanese business texts often speak of avoiding the three M's: *muri, mura,* and *muda*. Overextending beyond one's capacity is called *muri*; doing work unevenly and producing materials which do not befit specifications is called *mura*; and the third, wastefulness, is called *muda*. Being too adventuresome or shooting for the moon is a no-no in business, and so is wasting money, employees' talent, and time. Uneven work habits and products lead to loss of market share for the company.

In contrast, when a company has a corporate atmosphere where employees can communicate with each other freely, and work toward a common goal, that company will succeed.[1]

During the eighties, when Japan was basking in the glory of "Japan as Number One," I was privileged to visit over 120 Japanese companies. Those companies which were considered superior held several features in common. They all had a clear-cut and easy-to-understand corporate philosophy, they had a good program to train and educate their employees, and their internal communication was smooth and pleasant. During the same period, I was asked to visit a number of small and mid-size businesses in the United States. What struck me at that time was very few of the American companies had a corporate philosophy of their own. I surmised at that time that this lack of a viable corporate philosophy was one

---

1. Japanese business textbooks have a special word, *kazedooshi*, which means "ventilation."

Solution II: Learning from Business Practices

of the factors that made the US lose her competitiveness against Japan.[2]

Corporate philosophy has a long tradition in Japan. In 1694, the founder of the Mitsui department store decreed that "members of the family shall not fight against one another," and that "luxury is strictly forbidden and without fail saving must be enforced."[3] Earlier in 1660, the founder of the Sumitomo mining fortune gave this precept: "Do not purchase an article offered below the prevailing market price, whatever it is, without knowing its origin, regard such an article as stolen."[4] The spirits of these precepts are preserved as corporate philosophies for Mitsui and Sumitomo today. We have a great deal to learn from this if we want our church planting to succeed.

Before we start church planting we must determine our purpose and set our goals. The purpose is *Soli Deo Gloria*, so it can be easily settled. As for the goals, disputes may arise. Let us now take one step a time.

STEP 1. SETTING GOALS (DRAFT GUIDELINES)

1. Setting goals is the responsibility of the minister and elders. The session must meet to determine these goals. It must consider the needs of the community, the church's ability to meet these needs, which needs must be prioritized, and which population group must be the main focus of evangelization. Elders will draft a proposal and share that with those who are interested in church planting in order to gather their opinions. Hereafter this shall be called draft guidelines.

---

2. For disclosure, I taught a course entitled "Business with Japan," and visits to Japanese companies were made for the purpose of collecting materials for this course. Visits to American companies were sometimes done on a consulting basis. My findings are given in my book *Inside Corporate Japan: The Art of Fumble-Free Management* (Cambridge, MA: Productivity, 1987).

3. Mitsui founder's precept is available in https://kakunist.jimdo.com/2015/10/02/. My translation.

4. Lu, *Japan*, 239.

2. At the next session meeting, elders will report the opinions gathered, and consider the formation of a church planting team most suited for meeting these goals. .

3. The following Sunday, the minister will give a sermon on the importance of church planting and ask members of the congregation for their support. People who are interested in joining the church planting team are encouraged to communicate their wishes to the session.

The ultimate goal of church planting is to produce a daughter church. Lack of mentioning it here is deliberate. Some Japanese churches are small, and may feel that they have neither time nor money to think about church planting. But the fact is that a small church can do church planting also. The key lies in what one considers the word "church" to mean.

Church is not a building. In Jesus' time, to be in church was to be with Jesus. It could be under the blue sky or over the raging Sea of Galilee under a storm. If we do not think of church in terms of having its own building, small churches can also aspire to do church planting. It can make plans to lead others to his invisible church, and it can help set up house churches in remote rural areas.

I once attended a Sunday service in Shanghai in a church built by the British people who had once occupied the city's foreign concessions. The church was commodious, with an impressive pipe organ. It was, however, sparsely attended. There were Chinese people wanting to enter, but were prevented by the police. In that same China, the number of Christians increases day after day. They conduct their services in homes where some of them do not even have electricity. They lack edifices, but they still have their churches in their homes and in their hearts.

STEP 2. SELECTING CHURCH PLANT TEAM MEMBERS

1. Team members are volunteers. However, they do represent their church and their appointment must be approved by the session. The criteria can be found in the following passage:

Solution II: Learning from Business Practices

> Deacons likewise must be serious, not double tongued, not indulging in much wine, not greedy for money; they must hold fast to the mystery of the faith with a clear conscience. And let them first be tested; then, if they prove themselves blameless, let them serve as deacons. Women likewise must be serious, not slanderers, but temperate, faithful in all things. Let deacons. . . manage their children and their households well; for those who serve well as deacons gain a good standing for themselves and great boldness in the faith that is in Christ Jesus. (2 Tim 3:8–12)[5]

2. Missionaries from overseas may join as members of the church planting team. It is important to find people, men and women alike, from various walks of life to join the team who can effectively answer the needs of the local community. To nurture future leaders of the church, pay special attention to having a young person join. Examine your draft guidelines and if you are targeting families who have mixed religions, be sure to have members from such families join your team.

3. The responsibility for church planting rests on the entire congregation. Opinions will differ, and so will actions. Remember the Japanese term *kazedooshi* to keep information flowing smoothly within the organization. That is one important function the church planting team is expected to perform. On the basis of the draft guidelines set by the session, the team must prepare its own short-term goals and long-term goals, and submit them to the session.

4. Team members must know what other members are doing. They must maintain close contact with one another, not by e-mail and phone only, but also through regularly scheduled meetings. Don't be too polite and unable to speak up. Foreign members must

---

5. Here I have used The New Revised Standard Version to allow the word "women" to be used in verse 11 to emphasize that women can become active members of a church planting team. The word "women" here in the original Greek can either be translated as "women" or "wives." It is not my intention in this book to engage in the discussion of the propriety of ordination of women as deacons.

Overcoming Barriers to Evangelization in Japan

learn to ask the right questions. Please don't give your co-workers the impression that foreigners are incapable of understanding the Japanese mind.

5. A regularly scheduled meeting provides a forum where members can exchange notes and help each other to correct mistakes and avoid recurrences. It is also a forum where they can jointly investigate new opportunities and approaches. To help your discussion go smoothly and find common ground, try to use the cause-and-effect diagram introduced below:

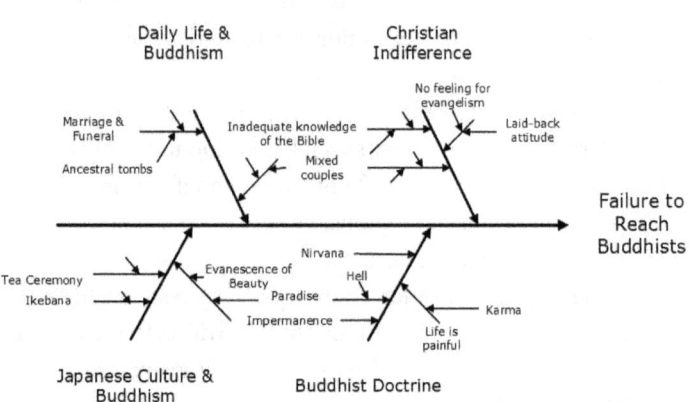

Cause & Effect Diagram

HOW TO USE THE CAUSE-AND-EFFECT DIAGRAM

One of the key functions engineers engage in is called process control. Manufacturers want to eliminate defects from their products by standardization, but there are so many cause factors to consider. "The cause factors which will influence effects are not many,"[6] Most engineers knew this, but they had difficulty identifying these factors. In 1952, while working for Kawasaki Iron Works, Dr. Ishikawa Kaoru invented the cause-and-effect diagram to identify the two or three most important factors. Its use allowed the company to successfully control them. Since then, the diagram

---

6. Kaoru Ishikawa, *What is Total Quality Control?: The Japanese Way.* Translated by David J. Lu (Englewood Cliffs, NJ: Prentice Hall, 1985), 64.

Solution II: Learning from Business Practices

has been adopted for use worldwide, not just in manufacturing, but in situations totally unrelated to manufacturing.

Ishikawa explains the utility and success of his diagram in the following terms: "In searching for these important cause factors, people who are familiar with a particular process, such as workers, engineers, and researchers, must all be consulted. They must be able to discuss the process openly and frankly, and the session can be conducted as a brainstorming session."[7]

It is not difficult to use the cause-and-effect diagram. First draw a wide and bold line from left to right on a black (or white) board. At the end of the line signified by an arrow, the man on duty for the day will write down the day's topic. Let us say that "Why have we not been able to reach Buddhists?" is the day's topic which is put up on the board. Other members each will have an idea of why. They each will put that idea either above or below the bold line, and then draw a line diagonally left to right toward the bold center line. If there are similar ideas they can be merged into one line. If ideas are only slightly different, the group can decide which shall be the main and which shall become an auxiliary line. There can be as many auxiliary lines as needed. You have to try it once in order to know how easy it is to use. It is a wonderful tool to get the discussion going.

When your team is putting their heads together to decide the goals to be pursued, you can use this diagram to sort things out. Church planting team members often have to work alone. You can utilize this diagram to merge your individual experiences into one commonly shared experience for the group. Similarities can easily be found through the lines drawn, difficulties will also be shared in this manner and so will the solutions.

I have witnessed Dr. Ishikawa using this diagram to train employees of various companies, turning a good company into a recipient of the coveted Deming Prize. As a translator of his book, I was asked by American companies to help them apply his methods for quality improvement. In each case, what I saw was how easily this diagram could be used for brainstorming. In Japan's

---

7. Ishikawa, *What is Total Quality Control?*, 64.

Overcoming Barriers to Evangelization in Japan

hierarchical settings, normally subordinate members do not dare speak up. However, when they are using this diagram, they will draw the lines confidently, and speak with pride about their discoveries. It is a simple, yet remarkably effective tool. I hope you will be able to use it for church planting.

STEP 3. IMPLEMENTATION TEAMS

When a company wishes to improve quality, full participation by all employees is the key to its success. This is also true with church planting. Its success depends on the willingness of the entire congregation to participate in this worthwhile endeavor. Implementation teams are created for that purpose. Participation is voluntary, and there is no restriction on the number of teams to be formed. Teams will consist of people who are members of the church and are interested in evangelism. They must agree to follow the draft guidelines established by the session and receive the necessary training. Otherwise they are welcome to use their imagination and instinct. They must, however, agree to meet regularly with fellow members of the team, and report their activities to the church planting team.

STEP 4. CHURCH'S SELF EXAMINATION

"The greatest factor in Christianity not being accepted in Japan has always been considered in the realm of the political and historical background. Making that conclusion does not advance our discussion," says theologian Sakurai Kunio. "To me, the most serious cause has always been the prevailing notion held within the Christian community that 'Christianity does not stand a chance of being accepted in Japan.'"[8] This says a lot about the current status of Christianity in Japan.

---

8. Sakurai Kunio, *Ikyo toshiteno Kirisutokyo karano Dakkyaku* (Escape from Christianity as an Alien Religion) (Tokyo: Revival Shimbun, 2004), 4

Solution II: Learning from Business Practices

In the beginning of this book, I have suggested that "self" is the first barrier preventing acceptance of Christianity in Japan. The self includes our churches. Unless we can overcome this barrier, we cannot successfully plant churches. After Christ was crucified, "the veil of the temple was torn in two from top to bottom" (Mark 15:18). The old had passed away, and it signaled the beginning of a new era. If we want to succeed in church planting we must tear ourselves away from old thinking that has bound us to inaction.

Have you ever seriously thought about the future of the 500,000 mission school graduates each year? A majority of them are women, and once they are married their connection with the Christian community ceases. Have you ever tried to reach out to them? Take a look within your own congregation. A number of your members are married to non-Christians. Have you ever tried to talk to their spouses? Have you ever tried to reach out to their children? Churches have been complacent on many of these issues.

Church members represent a variety of professions. They must ask themselves: Am I a Sunday Christian who attends Sunday services regularly, but forgets about Christ once he leaves the door of the church?

Japan is a vertical society with a rigid hierarchical structure. If the minister does not move, the congregation will not move. If that happens, the minister must repent of his ways. I know of a small church of less than 250 members in the United States that has, in the past decade, successfully planted two daughter churches. Its minister has always encouraged church members to consider themselves as ministers. The church bulletin has printed it, and his and associate minister's names are referred to only as teaching elders. Its church planting activities were fully supported by the entire congregation. The humility of its ministers and full participation by the congregation were keys to its success.

The importance of each lay member's active participation in church planting cannot be overemphasized. Early Christianity spread very rapidly. Behind the remarkable works of the apostles was the support rendered by the new converts. For example: "Epaphras, who is one of you, a bondservant of Christ, greets you, always laboring fervently for you in prayers, that you may stand perfect and complete in all the will of God. For I bear him witness that he has a great zeal for you"(Col 4:12–13). Paul could not have done what he did without the help of those people who tirelessly supported him. We seldom read Paul's postscripts. But when you are discouraged with something, read some of these postscripts. The apostles faced many difficulties very much like what you are experiencing today. Try to emulate the apostles and experience the joy they felt when they received help from their new converts.

Acts records this unusual event in Paul's ministry: "And in a window sat a certain young man named Eutychus, who was sinking into a deep sleep. He was overcome by sleep, and as Paul continued speaking, he fell down from the third story and was taken up dead" (Acts 20:9). We must be awakened from the sleep of "Christianity does not stand a chance of being accepted in Japan."

If we are satisfied with only one percent of the entire Japanese population being Christians, we are no different from this wicked and lazy servant: "Then he who had received the one talent came and said, 'Lord, I knew you to be a hard man, reaping where you have not sown, and gathering where you have not scattered seed. And I was afraid, and went and hid your talent in the ground. Look there you have what is yours'"(Matt 25:24–25).

After the session has discussed and pondered the issue of church planting, it will be good for the minister to give a sermon on this topic.

STEP 5. COLLECTING LOCAL INFORMATION

We have taken care of the first barrier, but there are four still remaining. Unless we obtain accurate information about these four barriers surrounding our community, we will not be able to eliminate them. The first task we have is to collect information.

This task is to be performed by as many members of the congregation as possible. Sunday school, Bible study groups, ladies associations, etc., are all encouraged to take part. Now let us find the most efficient way of collecting local information.

Solution II: Learning from Business Practices

1. It will depend on the size and preference of the church, but my suggestion is to create four teams in addition to the church planting team.[9] These four teams will each specialize in one of the barriers discussed in this book. If the church is small and unable to form these four separate teams, assign four members of the church planting team to become collectors of information about four barriers, with each given responsibility for one barrier.

2. Whenever a church member obtains information, he will communicate that to the team or person responsible for that specific barrier.

3. The four information-gathering teams shall be named according to the four barriers for which they are responsible: Buddhism, Shintoism, Humanism, and Social Ills. These four teams must periodically meet, use the cause-and-effect diagram to analyze, and submit their findings to the church planting team.

4. Consider your own church as one of the local institutions from which information must be collected. Your members can supply on a voluntary basis the names of their loved ones who are not Christians who need prayers and church care. If done well, this will become one of the keys toward the church's own revitalization.

Collecting information about one's own community is not a difficult task. It is a familiar territory. The only difference is that church members now have a mission to perform, and their eyes and ears will be more attuned to the surroundings. Take, for example, Buddhism: a person may have not paid much attention to the Buddhist temple in the neighborhood, but now that he has to collect information for his church, he may decide to enter the gate of the temple. In the temple garden, there are a number of stone lanterns with names of donors carved into the side. There he may find the names of his neighbors' ancestors. If he is adventuresome, he can seek to meet with the temple priest, and will be surprised how easily it can be arranged. In this way he will establish a point of contact for his church. In a Shinto shrine, one can use a similar approach to obtain information.

---

9. These information-gathering teams can be separate from, or overlap with. implementation teams as discussed earlier.

Overcoming Barriers to Evangelization in Japan

Going to a school board meeting, or to a parent-teacher meeting can provide other useful information. Visits to local government offices and self-governing volunteer organizations are also a must. Hospitals, old people's homes, and police stations, etc., must also be visited to collect information.

Previously we cited Tim Keller, who spoke about the importance of the church owning the neighborhood. Information gathering allows us to become one with our community. We own the knowledge of their needs, and they become our needs to attend to.

STEP 6. SHORT-TERM AND LONG-TERM GOALS

The church planting team, once it has completed analysis of the data collected, will start drafting short-term and long-term goals, the latter expressing the hopes of the entire congregation. Please include in your long-term goals the following passage from the *Westminster Confession of Faith*, Chapter 25. Article 1:

> The catholic or universal church, which is invisible, consists of the whole number of the elect, that have been, are, or shall be gathered into one, under Christ the head thereof; and is the spouse, the body, the fullness of him that filleth all in all.

Inclusion of this passage is to serve as a reminder that when things are not going well, our ultimate goal is to be gathered to this invisible church, and that being the case, the visible church which we are trying to construct on this earth may not have to be in the form or shape that we have first envisioned.

Committee members are encouraged to discuss among themselves the ideal size for their own church, and their consensus figure must be included in the long-term goals. Once your church reaches that size, it becomes the time to work actively to plant a daughter church.

The task of drafting short-term goals comes up next. In this document, the team must place emphasis on what is doable, creating a healthy plan which will not overtax the church's available

Solution II: Learning from Business Practices

resources. In the preceding chapters of this book, I have noted that the following tools are available for creating contact with non-Christians. Please incorporate one or more of these tools in your short-term goals to examine their practicability:

Tea ceremony or *ikebana* school

Support for home-school-type *juku*

Home Bible study groups

Informal gatherings in church with non-Christians

Church as a culture center for the community

Setting up a counseling center in the church

These are merely suggestions. They may or may not fit into your plan. After you try them out, please use the cause-and-effect diagram to make assessment and necessary adjustments.

HOUSE CHURCH

Holding worship services in private homes has been a key factor in the spread of Christianity in China. It is a tool Japanese Christians must actively consider. Heretofore, I have avoided raising this issue because of many valid reasons given by missionaries and friends. Some objections to the idea of a house church are: "The national character of the Japanese people is different from that of the Chinese. They do not like to congregate in a private home"; "The house is small and there is not enough space in the neighborhood for cars to park"; "Family honor requires that the house be cleaned spick and span before receiving guests."[10] They all are

---

10. On this particular point, Bob Drews, the Tokyo team leader of MTW, sent me this comment: "There was, perhaps twenty years ago, a great measure of enthusiasm regarding House Church from within the missionary community. I am told the Southern Baptist mission determined that House Church would be their sole strategy. There are still some missionaries practicing House Church in Japan. The movement turned out not to have as much power as it has had in China, perhaps for some of the reasons you list. There are still House Churches, and groups promoting house church. Some of these groups

good reasons, but in my mind's eye I have a contrasting image. It was around the turn of the century when I was invited to visit a Chinese family in Beijing. We went up three stories without an elevator. The passageway leading to their apartment was without light. There, in a room with only one light bulb burning, they were holding their worship service.

Paul's letter to Colossians contains this passage: "Greet the brethren who are in Laodicea, and Nymphas and the church that is in his house" (Col 4:15). Churches did not own separate property for worship until the middle of the third century. Without the hospitality extended by those early believers who provided space for house church, the early church could not have spread the way it did.

To be successful, the church planting team must depart from conventional wisdom. I am firmly convinced that house churches can become an effective tool in Japan. In the late eighties, I served a year as director of Associated Kyoto Program, which is a consortium of twelve colleges for Japanese studies attached to Doshisha University. I had fifty-two students who were all placed with Japanese families. Host families knew each other well, because many of them had done that for many years. They often invited each other to their homes along with their student guests. One day I thanked one of the home-stay mothers, commenting that it was such a rare thing to have a large party held in a private home. "Oh, it's nothing really," she answered, "When Americans are involved, it is much easier to have a party. We don't have to worry about *omiyage* (taking a gift to the host) or *okaeshi* (providing a return gift)."

Could it be that this social convention called *omiyage* and *okaeshi* has prevented Japanese Christians from setting up house churches? It is worth raising this issue with your congregation. If you already have a group holding Bible study at home, they may not be averse to holding a worship service in their home as well.

House churches are far more approachable than regular churches. There is no implied commitment to become a Christian,

---

go beyond my understanding of how churches should be constituted." E-mail dated September 17, 2018.

Solution II: Learning from Business Practices

nor is there anything to worry about with respect to a dress code, for example. This ease of access is especially important for those who are underprivileged. In the sixties, the Rev. and Mrs. Nakamori[11] had a ministry for the homeless and lived in a row house among the poorest of the poor in Asakusa, Tokyo. Every morning he would take *omusubi* (rice balls) made by his wife to the homeless and invited them to come to worship with him at his house on Sunday. On Sundays they came filling his two *tatami* rooms and the veranda. They listened to his sermon and sang with him hymns led by his strong baritone voice which was always off key. Worshippers were not the same every Sunday, but they would spread the word among themselves. They knew from where they could get *omusubi* and the word of God that satiated their spiritual hunger. The Nakamori house became an oasis for the homeless. They came to wash their clothing and bathed in their backyard. In an emergency they would take shelter there, but never overstayed their welcome. The comings and goings of the homeless infested their house with bed bugs. The Nakamoris endured it as another sign of God teaching them how to live among the poor, and continued their daily routine of serving the Lord.

The Nakamori model would not work in today's Japan. With urban renewal, all traces of his old neighborhood are gone. Did the Nakamoris successfully plant a church there? Yes, they did, in the hearts and minds of the men and women they served. "The catholic or universal church, which is invisible, consists of the whole number of the elect." It was that church that the Nakamoris planted. It is worth remembering that the church was, is not, and never will be just a building.

Having said all of this, I have been reminded that there was a house church which was begun in a war widow's living room in Yokkaichi which was offered to a newly arrived MTW missionary couple Bruce and Susan Young shortly after the war. It became a

---

11. Nakamori Ikunoshin (1904–1981) was a Methodist pastor. I visited him in November 1965 and was able to observe his ministry firsthand. He accepted his Asakusa pastorate, which effectively cut his salary down to one-third of his previous pay. His experiences were recorded in his autobiography *Shita e Noboru Uta (A Song of Climbing to the Bottom)* (1973).

Presbyterian church, which planted many daughter churches that became the core of the newly organized Presbyterian Church in Japan, now affiliated with PCA.[12] God works wonders in so many different ways.

We shall now go back to Step 6 about short-term and long-term goals. Sort-term goals are to serve as an operating manual for the church planting team. It must set a deadline for attaining these goals in two or three months. After these goals are met, the team will draft new short-term goals incorporating previous experiences. This process must be repeated two or three times, before the team can revise the long-term goals. There will come a time when the team feels that the work they have been doing must be performed by the entire congregation. It is at this point that they will make the final revision. The revised long-term goals must be submitted to the session.

Reading the above paragraphs, you may feel that I am giving cumbersome regulations. No, they are not regulations. What is written is from business consulting experiences to make certain that internal communication flows smoothly. Do not take these paragraphs as stiff regulations. Please revise everything written here to suit your purpose.

STEP 7. MINISTER AND SESSION

The session will examine the long-term goals from the standpoint of (1) the entire congregation, and (2) the financial cost to be incurred. It will probe every aspect carefully, make corrections, and if there is no dissent, give its approval. Once the document is approved, it must be distributed to the entire congregation. At this point the responsibility for church planting is transferred to the shoulders of the entire congregation. The team will not dissolve and continue to serve as the nerve center for information gathering. At this juncture, the team is encouraged to give an in-depth report to the entire congregation.

---

12. https://www.youtube.com/watch?v=efx1OB_ziHs

Solution II: Learning from Business Practices

However, the following two functions remain the responsibility of the session:

1. Obtaining adequate funding for the daughter church.
2. Selecting a minister for the daughter church.

There are several ways to obtain adequate funding. One can always ask for special donations. However, the surest way is to designate each year a set percentage of budget for church planting. The accumulated amount can then be turned over to the daughter church when it is formed. For this reason too, it is essential that church planting must have full participation from all its members.

Have you ever thought of receiving contributions by other churches? If other churches belong to the same denomination, there is not likely to be any problem. Now, however, will you be willing to accept donations from churches other than from your own denomination?

There are several factors to take into account.

First, in Japan, most churches still belong to the United Church of Christ in Japan (UCCJ) which was formed under pressure from the military in 1941. After the war, a number of denominations parted company with UCCJ which included the Reformed church in Japan. However, there are still a significant number of churches with Reformed persuasion remaining with UCCJ. One of such is Shiloh Church in Yokohama, established by Dr. James Hepburn.

Second, most Japanese churches are small in size and on their own will not be able to shoulder the financial burden of establishing a daughter church.

Given these two factors, I do not see any basis for refusing contributions from churches with the same persuasion even though they may still belong to UCCJ. In fact I would like to urge missionaries to seek out churches with the same persuasion and work with them to promote church planting.

Let us consider a case of a small town that has no church. Your denomination is interested in planting one there and there is another denomination which does not always agree with you

Overcoming Barriers to Evangelization in Japan

doctrinally. Will you be willing to cooperate with them? You have to let your conscience be your guide, and pray for his guidance. However, I hope you will put the interest of the targeted town first, and ask yourself this question: Will the doctrinal differences matter that much in the invisible church in heaven? My own inclination is to move forward and work with the other denomination to plant a church in that town.[13]

Laos is a country still governed by a Communist government, and where Christianity is severely restricted. My son and daughter-in-law were there serving as medical missionaries for a number of years. There were less than twenty missionaries in Vientiane, its capital, representing six or seven nations and as many denominations. I was in one of their meetings where prayers were given, meals were taken, and common problems faced were discussed. Differences in doctrine were not an issue among them. They were all eager to preach the gospel in the manner they understood it. When one is placed in the sea of nonbelievers, one comes to the realization that we all worship the same God and depend on the same Savior. In Japan, we face a situation where 99 percent of its people still do not accept Christ. Oftentimes it is best to put our differences aside, and work with those who may not always agree with us.

Let us take a moment to think about our denominational affiliation and the manner in which we present our views to our Japanese friends. Of course, we can proudly proclaim our Reformed heritage, but that cannot be done at the expense of our Christian unity. We have one Lord, one baptism, and before we are Presbyterians, Reformed, or anything else, we are all Christians. Try to see this from the perspectives of our Japanese friends. They come to us to seek Christ. If we insist on expounding our theological differences constantly, we alienate them and drive them away from Christ. Uchimura Kanzo's (1861–1930) nonchurch movement was

---

13. For disclosure, I attended Westminster Theological Seminary and currently belong to a conservative church affiliated with the Presbyterian Church in America. However, I once served as an elder in a church affiliated with the Presbyterian Church USA, which is not a conservative denomination.

Solution II: Learning from Business Practices

started as a reaction against incessant doctrinal disputes among foreign missionaries. From there he attempted to develop a distinct Japanese Christianity in which Japanese values would be fused with those of Christianity. Today we speak of contextualization. His was such an attempt and is worthy of our attention. As for the nonchurch movement itself, it has become a significant intellectual force, impacting academia, peace, and social justice movements.[14]

Choosing a minister is always difficult, and when it comes to choosing a new pastor for a daughter church, the difficulty will compound. The daughter church lacks resources and does not have an established pool of regular contributors. Not many candidates will be attracted to it. It will be unwise to appoint a person with several young children to a financially strapped daughter church and expect him to perform well. A single person will fit the bill much better. If a minister cannot be found, establishing a daughter church may have to be postponed. Or you can make an arrangement with a local minister to fill in the pulpit until a suitable minister can be found. Of course in that case the worship hour has to be changed. There is, however, a third way: One minister may be appointed to two pastorates. He can give his sermon in one church, and have it skyped to another. This can be alternated between the two congregations.

Many successful church plants in America have been accomplished by the mother church sending its own associate pastor to the daughter church. That is one model Japanese churches can follow.

Finding a building to start a church in is also difficult, but let us begin by remembering that church is not a building. If someone in your church is sent overseas for three to six months, worship services can be held in that apartment for that length of time.

---

14. Uchimura's criticism of foreign missionaries, though dated, can still be used as a guide for missionaries to engage in self-evaluation. See John Howe *Japan's Modern Prophet: Uchimura Kanzo, 1861–1930* (Vancouver: University of British Columbia Press, 2005). From its inception in 1878 through today, Tokyo University has had thirty-four presidents, and two of them belonged to the nonchurch movement.

Department stores are losing customers and their restaurants are severely underutilized. You can rent that space for two hours each Sunday morning to conduct your services. In local areas, some movie theaters are no longer in business. Their space can also be utilized. If everything else fails, there is still the neighborhood coffee shop. Use your imagination.

Incidentally, have you ever thought of renting a conference room from your neighborhood company for your Sunday morning worship? Most companies are well-located, easily accessible, and provide parking facilities.

WHAT GOALS TO EMPHASIZE?

So far we have been borrowing from business practices to show how church planting should be operated. However, we have been silent on the goals we wish to reach. For long-term goals, we must envision a large picture: Where do we plan to establish daughter churches? Which people are we trying to attract? What steps do we need to take and why are they important? A long-term financial commitment must be included in these goals, e.g., we will set aside 5 percent of our annual budget for X number of years to establish a daughter church.

Short-term goals usually contain mundane matters, e.g., we will concentrate on reaching non-Christian spouses of mixed couples, or we will establish a training course for church planting during the Sunday school hours for the next eight weeks.

Long- and short-term goals complement one another. If long-term goals contain the following: "Each member of this congregation must pledge that in his lifetime, he will bring at least one person to Christ," short-term goals can respond by adding the following: "In the coming three months, each church member is expected to invite a friend to come to an event sponsored by this church."

Here let us reflect again on Jesus' last injunction: "Go therefore and make disciples of all the nations" (Matt 28:19). What does it mean to us, who are mostly urban dwellers?:

Solution II: Learning from Business Practices

1. Adopting rural villages as church planting targets: Just as America is not New York, Los Angeles, and Chicago, Japan is not Tokyo, Osaka, and Nagoya. In rural Japan, there are many towns and villages that do not have a single church within them. It will be good for our churches to adopt some of them in our prayers and consider them as future targets for church planting. We do not neglect church planting in our own community, but this adoption will allow us to extend our mission nationwide in scope. The rural areas to be adopted are not chosen at random, but through a survey of the congregation about their rural ties. The needs of a specific area and the number of people having ties to that specific area are factors to be considered in selection. Once areas are selected, encourage your members to set up a mission trip to these unchurched areas. It will give them a chance to become missionaries without leaving Japan. The experience they bring back from these mission trips will also make them better church planters. We call it a multiplier effect: one blessing leads to another.

2. The phrase "all the nations" includes all generations. Just as the invisible church "consists of the whole number of the elect that have been, are, or shall be," the visible church consists of all age groups. In church planting we must always be mindful of the importance of nurturing leaders of the next generation. Once that becomes our goal, if there is a college nearby, we will become more mindful of how to make our church friendlier to college students. We can help them select their future occupation in a way that is pleasing to God. Church planting is a process. Each step we take, God will show us how to advance to the next step. It is with that assurance we all must endeavor

Jesus has honored all of us who walk with him as ones greater than John the Baptist (Matt 11:11).[15] Armed with this blessing he has bestowed on us, we can claim victory for his kingdom in Japan.

---

15. See Keller, *Center Church*, 345.

Epilogue

Good and Faithful Church Planter

A DESIRABLE CHURCH PLANTER is one who walks with the Lord, has compassion for lost sheep, respects friendship, is adaptable to his surroundings, is not self-serving, is patient, has good knowledge of the Bible and learns from it, and has a passion for sharing it with others.

This list would not be complete without adding John Mehn's six-interrelated characteristics. They are: "God-given vision, risk-taking faith, an organic view of the church, developing lay people, encouraging leadership style, and aggressive implementation."[1] Here are some more factors to consider.

DON'T BE DISCOURAGED WHEN THINGS DON'T TURN OUT RIGHT

"A lot of young people came to our concert last night. We invited them to come to our church. We were all excited. But when we

---

1. Dr. John Mehn, author of *Multiplying Churches in Japanese Soil* (William Cary Library, 2017) is a missionary in Japan of long standing and conducts seminars for church planters. His findings cited above are based on a survey of forty-three churches. I am grateful to him for giving me access to his research data.

opened the door to our church this morning, no young person showed up—only a few grandpas and grandmas." This is an extreme case. In reality some young people will come. But here is the point: once the door of the church is open, don't pick and choose who comes in. True, the concert was planned to attract young people and it did not work out that way. However, there are people who came and they are seeking God. Be thankful that an opportunity is given to you to serve them.

And speaking of holding a concert, the following words of Hudson Taylor are worth remembering:

"Do not have your concert first, and then tune your instrument afterwards. Begin the day with the word of God and prayer, and get first of all into harmony with him."[2]

ALLOW DISSENT AND LISTEN TO OTHERS

We all agree that we seek *Soli Deo Gloria*, but when it comes to its implementation, people do not always agree. It becomes a source of frustration and even contention. Ministers and session members may feel betrayed: "We have crafted this plan prayerfully. Why can't they see that?" Among the church members, there are eager beavers who feel that church is not doing enough and there are others who resent the way things are handled. It is not easy to be a minister or a missionary. However, you must realize that through these trials, God is training you to become a better and more effective servant of his. Learn to be a patient listener. Dissenters do have their points. Find out why they hold onto a vision different from yours. In church planting we are navigating many uncharted territories. Show your willingness to follow the dissenters' vision. In fact theirs might even work out better than your own vision. Your willingness to listen to them will make them more willing to listen to you. Your congregation and the church planting team will all be strengthened by that.

---

2. From https://www.goodreads.com/author/quotes/4693730.James_Hudson_Taylor, para. 2.

The above statement is applicable to Japanese ministers and to their congregation. For missionaries, listening to your Japanese colleagues is doubly important. Listen to them carefully and let them make their points. They can contextualize your ideals to the Japanese people far better than you can do it on your own!

TATEMAE AND *HONNE*

In Japan, people are trained to speak carefully to please others. There is a phrase called "*tatemae* and *honne*" that goes to the heart of Japanese behavior. *Tatemae* is a public stance, what one is expected to say in public, and *honne* is what one really feels, and containing his true intention. For the Japanese, this has never been an issue. They know exactly what the other party is thinking and they can act accordingly. But for foreigners it creates a veil of mystery.

Put this in the context of your work. Let us say that you have organized a plan to reach out to a certain group, and your Japanese co-workers tell you that the plan is working well. The number does not verify it. It does not mean that your Japanese colleagues are lying to you. They are simply being polite. In their minds, they know the plan does not work, but they cannot say it out loud.

So the first order of business is to ask your Japanese colleagues to say things with *honne*. But they are not likely to quickly getting out of the habit of speaking with *tatemae*. Your plan B is to keep on asking questions, until you get an answer consistent with external data.

There is, however, a better way to train your Japanese colleagues to speak with *honne*. Share with them stories about the mistakes you have made. Let them know that to point out the mistakes you have committed is actually an act of kindness. Sharing stories of mistakes made has another salutary effect. Colleagues become friends, and the shared knowledge of mistakes each has committed will more clearly show the right path to take next time.

DON'T TAKE A SHORTCUT

Establishing a new church is to create a new organization. It takes time to sort out all kinds of unexpected problems that arise. Each of them has to be solved one by one. Taking time means to solidify the results. The cohesiveness of a new organization can come only through this process.

> The Lord said to Joshua: 'I have given Jericho into your hand... You shall march around the city, all you men of war; you shall go all around the city once. This you shall do six days... But the seventh day you shall march around the city seven times... and when you hear the sound of the trumpet, that all the people shall shout with a great shout; then the wall of the city will fall down flat" (Josh 6:2–5).

In that tropical land, soldiers with heavy armor were told by God to march round and round the city seven times. It would almost sound cruel. If God wanted it, Jericho would have fallen in a day. But he had a purpose, a lesson to teach the people of Israel. To enter and live in God's promised land, people must not be overanxious, and must learn to depend on God's grace to live.

SOMETIMES IT IS GOOD TO GIVE UP

The three M's, trying to attain something unreachable, unevenness in workmanship, and waste are frowned upon by businesses. In church planting, the same principles apply. Jesus teaches us in the parable of the sower that we must seek "the good ground" to sow. Seed cast on the wayside, sown on stony places, and among the thorns cannot grow (Matt 13:18–23). When you are setting up your goals, be sure to prioritize carefully. During the implementation stage, you may find some projects are simply unworkable. In such instances, it may be necessary to abandon that particular project. When deciding whether to abandon or not to abandon, pray for guidance and use the cause-and-effect diagram to determine your course of action.

Overcoming Barriers to Evangelization in Japan

FEAR NOTHING, FOR THE LORD IS WITH YOU

You are in Japan because you love the Lord and Japan. So with prayers and supplications proceed without fear. "The only thing we have to fear is fear itself" said FDR in his first inaugural address. That was the first step the nation had to take to recover from the worst depression ever experienced. The Philadelphia Eagles had always been an underdog until 2018 when it won its first Super Bowl. When asked how he coached this team, Doug Pederson answered: "Fear nothing. Not our opponents, not failure, not anything in our lives."[3] It is a good piece of advice to follow in church planting as well.

MAGOKORO—HEART-TO-HEART FRIENDSHIP

The Japanese people cherish friendship that is built on the foundation of *magokoro*. The word "sincerity" comes closest to its meaning, but cannot express the feel *magokoro* conveys. Jonathan Edwards (1703–1758) spoke of "false piety, however spectacular, is evanescent and cannot endure; true piety, the sense of the heart, is an abiding foundation in the soul."[4] This true piety comes closest to what the Japanese people seek in *magokoro*. I hope you will be able to establish friendships on the basis of true piety. Your true piety will touch their hearts, and through it they will be able to experience the love of God with you.

REJOICING TO WALK WITH JESUS

You are a messenger of God's word in Japan. Sometimes you may feel powerless, lonely, and rejected. The word of God, however, will

---

3. Doug Perderson and Dan Pompei, "Inside Doug Perderson's Interview to Become Head Coach of the Philadelphia Eagles," para. 14. *Sports Illustrated* https://www.si.com/nfl/2018/08/20/doug-pederson-philadelphia-eagles-job-interview-fearless.

4. See John E. Smith, *Jonathan Edwards: Puritan, Preacher, Philosopher* (Notre Dame: University of Notre Dame Press, 1992), 33.

make you whole. "Come to Me, all you who labor and are heavy laden, and I will give you rest" (Matt 11:28).

So let us not fear and boldly spread his word across Japan: "For the word of God is living and powerful, and sharper than any two-edged sword, piercing even to the division of soul and spirit, and of joints and marrow, and is the discerner of the thoughts and intents of the heart" (Heb 4:12). That word turned Saul the persecutor into Paul the apostle. Saul was as to the Law, a Pharisee, a perfect 100 percent Hebrew of Hebrews. He cast aside all of that to become a faithful disciple of Christ. Among your friends, there are 100 percent good Buddhists, and 100 percent Shintoist believers. If you can bring just one of these people to Christ, Japan will come one step closer to the kingdom of God. Let us pray for that day to come.

God has given us the privilege of transmitting his word to another person. With that we have the joy of walking with God. If there is just one person we can lead to Christ, it will be a victory for God. "Blessed are the people who know the joyful sound! They walk, O Lord, in the light of your countenance" (Ps 89:15). "For your lovingkindness is before my eyes, and I have walked in your truth" (Ps 26:3).

According to the 2018 edition of the *Report of Japan's Religious Population*, 1.1 percent of Japanese people are Christians. However, this is not an accurate figure. Statistics given by the report show the total religious population to be at 181,164,731 as of January 1, 2018. The actual total population as of the same date was 126,587,000. The religious statistics contain double-counting of Buddhists and Shintoists. However, there is no double-counting of Christians. Since the total number of Christians was 1,921,804, percentagewise it comes out to 1.5 percent. If each Christian will bring one friend to Christ, that figure will double to 3 percent.[5] Let us pray that the day will come soon.

---

5. These figures are obtained from two Japanese government sources. They are: http://www.bunka.go.jp/tokei_hakusho_shuppan/hakusho_nenji-hokokusho/shukyo_nenkan/pdf/h30nenkan_gaiyo.pdf and https://www.stat.

Overcoming Barriers to Evangelization in Japan

May the Lord add his blessings to you as you toil for him in Japan.

Soli Deo Gloria.

---

go.jp/data/jinsui/new.html.

Name Index

Abraham, 66

Ballagh, James H., 72
Brown, Samuel R., 72

Calvin, John, 19, 89
Coe Sho-ki, 7f
Codevilla, Angelo M., 73
Confucius, 7f, 66, 71

Dogen, 16
Doshisha University, 106
Drews, Robert, 105f

Ebina Danjō, 5f
Edwards, Jonathan, 118
Eisai, 16

FDR, 118
Fukuzawa Yukichi, 29

Gramsci, Antonio, 74
Genshin, 14, 15, 25

Handel, 33
Heian Shrine 38, 40
Hepburn, James Curtis, 3–5, 45, 72
Hiei, Mt., 12
Hodge, Charles, 46
Honen, 15
Horyuji, 9

Inamori Kazuo, 32

Ise Shrine, 39
Ishikawa Kaoru, 98–99
Iwasaki Yataro, 29

Jacob, 51
Jerusalem, 72, 90–91

Kanto plain, 14
Kokugakuin University, 47
Konoye Fumimaro, 18
Karner, Linda, 62–64
Keelung, 60
Keller, Timothy, 80, 104
Kim, Lloyd H. 70f
Kiuchi Nobutane, 28–30, 76f
Kiuchi Sogoro, 66–67
Koya, Mt., 12
Kumamoto band, 5f
Kukai, 12
Kyoto, 12, 16, 21, 71
Kyoto Sangyo University, 64

Lansing, Janes, Leroy, 5–6, 7
Lowther, Roger, 50–51
Luther, Martin, 86, 87

Magellan, Ferdinand, 2–3
Masaoka Shiki, 9
Matsuo Basho, 10
Mehn, John, 114
Meiji Gakuin University, 3
Meiji Shrine 38, 39–40
Mishima Yukio, 32f

Name Index

Mission to the World (MTW), 62, 70, 107
Miura Ayako, 68
Motoori Norinaga, 44

Nagano Masao, 68
Nakamori Ikunoshin, 107
Nesbitt, Mariana, 67f
Newton, John, 89
Nichiren, 17
Nobutoki Kiyoshi, 37

Oda Nobunaga, 18
Okuno Masatsuna, 72
OMF international, 5
Otomo no Yakamochi, 37

Parry, Richard Lloyd, 49–50
Paul, 19, 26, 79, 91, 102, 119
Peter, 2, 72, 79, 85
Philadelphia Eagles, 118
Philip, 72
Pogo 1, 5

Rome, 78

Saicho, 12
Saigyo, 33
Saito Kazuo, 70

Sakurai Kunio, 100
Sato Eisaku, x, 29
Shanghai, 96
Shimada Hiromi, 83f
Showa, Emperor, 18
Sogoro, see Kiuchi Sogoro.

Taipei, 60
Taiwan, x, 60
Taylor, Hudson, 5, 115
Tokyo, x, 69, 76, 77
Tokyo University, 20, 46f, 65
Toyotomi Hideyoshi, 30
Timothy, 79
Tsuji Moriaki, 46f

Uemura Masahisa, 19
Uchimura Kanzo, 110–111
United Church of Christ in Japan (UCCJ), 109

Wang Yang-ming, 5

Xavier Francis, 30

Yanaihara Tadao, 20
Yasukuni shrine, 40
Young, Bruce and Susan, 107

Zhu Xi, 56

Subject Index

Alienation, 77
Amazing Grace, 89
Amida Buddha, 19, 20, 21, 33
Ancestry, 17, 32, 65
Ancestor worship, 38
Aristotelian logic 6, 36
Asceticism, 14, 90
Asia Harvest, 78
Atman (ultimate), 22
Aum Shinrikyo, 77

Ba'al, 46
Baptism 29, 35
Bakufu, 4, 14, 14f
Bible, 3, 27, 64–65, 79, 85
Bible study group, 47, 105
Bible times, 62–64
Bodhisattva, 12
Brahmanism, 22
Buddha, 12, 22
Buddha nature, 16
Buddhism, 9–36
    art, 9–10, 13, 23
    burial practices, 13, 28–30
    canon, 27,
    eschatology, see Mappo
    how to reach 98–99
    priest, 19, 20, 50
    reaction to PC, 75–76
    reformation, 14
    vs. State, 11, 18,
    temples, 31–32, 56

Bushido 5

Calligraphy 10
Catholic Church, 86, 87, 89
Cause and effect diagram, 98–100, 105,117
Census, religious 18, 41,119
China
    Buddhism in, 10–11, 16
    Christianity in, 66, 78, 96, 105, 106
    civilization, impact on Japan, 11, 12, 16, 58
Christianity
    ban on, 4, 30–31, 73
    early, 101
Church, 84, 86, 96
    early church 101–102, 106
    organization, 93–94, 107, 117
    self-examination, 6, 100–101, 102
Church planting, 87
    church plant team, 96–97, 103, 108
    congregation, 96–97,100, 101, 103, 108
    daughter church, 96 104, 108, 109,111
    goal setting, 95–96 choice, 112–113
    implementation team, 100, 103
    information gathering, 102–103

Subject Index

Church planting *(continued)*
   inter-denominational cooperation, 109–110
   long-term goals, 104, 108, 112–113
   minister's role, 96, 101,111, 115
   missionaries, 97 , 116
   session 96, 97, 102, 108, 115
   short-term goals, 104–105, 108, 112–113
   Information gathering, 102–104
Clan, see *uji*
Common grace, 21, 43
Community Arts Tokyo, 69–70
Confucian tradition, 4, 54–57
Confucianism, 54–55
Confucius 7f, 54–55, 66, 71
Contextualization, 6, 7, 10, 17–18, 43, 50–51, 63, 66–69, 116
Corporate philosophy, 94–95
Counseling center, 80–82, 105
Covenant, 66
Cross of Jesus, 20
Cultural center, church as, 69–70, 105
Cultural hegemony, 74–75, 78
Cultural heritage, 9–10

Death, 24, 26, 32, 33, 43
Denomination, 109–110

Easter, 34
Education
   Basic Act on, 53–54
   Higher, 12–13
   religious, 59
   under Tokugawa, 55
Emperor worship, 37–39
Emperor Showa, 18
   Humanity declaration, 38–39,40
Essentials for Salvation, 14
Examination hell, 58, 59
Exorcism, 50

Faith, (see also *Sola Fide*) 15, 20, 25
Family, 8, 17, 65–66, 68
Funeral, 28, 32

General revelation, 21
Genji, Tale of, 10
God, 45–46, 48
Ghost stories, 49–50
Ghosts of the Tsunami, 49–50
Good works 24 see also *jiriki*.
Grace, see *sola gratia*

Haiku, 9, 10
Handel's Messiah, 30, 63, 71
Heian period, 12-
Heian Shrine, 38, 40
Heidelberg Catechism, 26
Heike, Tale of, 10, 23
Hiei, Mt,. 12
Honne, 116
Home *juku*, 61–62,105
House church, 105–108
Hubris, 2
Humanism, 57–58
Humility, 3

Igime, 59
Ikebana, 10, 21,105
Imperial family, 10–11, 18
Impermanence of things, 23
Informal get-togethers, 34,105
Indulgence, 35, 86
Intermarriage, 8, 19, 27, 35,101
Invisible proscription, 78

Japanese
   art, 9
   gardening, 10,
   language, 4
   literature, 67–69
   painting, 10
   religious population, 18, 83, 119
Jiriki, 14
Jodo Shiu (Pure Land Sect), 15, 26

Subject Index

Juku, 59, 61 see also home *juku*, 105
Justification, 88

Hell, 14, 25

Kaimyo, 34
Kamakura period, 14–18
Kami, (Shinto deity) 41, 43–44, 45–46
Kana, 4, 13
Kanji, 4, 60
Karma, 21, 23, 24
Koan, 16
Kojiki, 43
Korea, 10
Koya, Mt., 12
Kukai, 12

Laos, missionaries in, 110
Latter Degenerate Days, see *Mappo*.
Layman's role, 35, 80–81, 82–83, 96–97, 100, 101, 114
Life, 23, 24, 25, 26, 53, 79–80, 81
Lotus Sutra, 17, 27
Luther, Martin, 86, 87

Mappo, 13, 14 17
Marriage, 28, 35
Meiji government, 18, 38
Meiji Shrine 38, 39–40
Migawari, 67, 68
Minister, 36, 102, 115
  in church planting, 96, 101
  definition, 3
Ministry tips, 35–36, 48–49, 50, 51–52, 60, 71–72
Mission schools, 28, 83, 101
Mission to the World, 62, 70, 107
Missionaries and daily life, 41, 47 48, 60–61
Mono no aware, 23

Nara, great Buddha, 11
Nara period, 10–12
Narrow Road of Oku, 10

National studies, 38
Nationalism, 39
Nature worship, 48–49
Nembutsu, 15
New morality, 76–77
Nichiren sect, 17, 77
Nirvana, 24
Non-church movement, 110–111
Northeast Japan disaster, 25,

Obon, 10
Ochugen, 10
Original vow, 20

Pain and suffering, 22, 23
Paradise, 20, 25, 26, 33
Penance, act of, 90
Perfectibility of man, 53–54, 57–58, 88
Political correctness, 73–75, 76–77, 82–84
Politics and religion, 10
Purification, 45
Rakugo, 70
Redemption, 49, 67, 77, 89
Reformation, 14, 34, 86, 87
Ren (仁)or jin (humanity), 54, 56
Repentance, 20
Rinzai sect, 15
Rissho Koseikai, 17, 77
Rural ministry, 113
Paradise, 14, 20, 25

Salvation, 15, 20, 24, 25, 35, 88
  plan of, 87, 91
Seeds of religion, 66
Self-denial, 6, 16, 23
Self-cultivation, 56
Self-reflection, 6, 100–101
Self-reliance, 14, 15, 16, 20, 58
Session, see Elder
Shame, 77
Shin Shiu or Jodo Shin Shiu, 15, 20
Shingon sect, 12, 14
Shiokari Pass, 68

Subject Index

Shinran, 15, 20, 25
Shinto, or Shintoism, 12, 37–51
  definition, 43–45
  festivals, 40–42
  purification, 45
  and state, 38
  studies 47
Shoen, 14
Shugendo, 90
Shushin, 56–57
Sin, 49, 88
Social convention, 106
Sola Scriptura, 85
Sola fide, 25, 87
Sola gratia, 24, 88
Soli Deo Gloria, 3, 24, 91–92, 95, 120
Solus Christus, 21, 24, 89
Soto sect, 15
Soul, 32
Sumo, 50–51
Soka Gakkai, 17, 77
Supreme Court, U. S., 75
Syncretism, 12, 38
Suicide, teen, 25–26, 59
Sun Goddess, 39
Sumo, 50–51
Syncretism, 12

Tohoku disaster, 49–50, 57
Taishō Revised Tripiṭaka, 27
Tannisho, 20

Taoism, 15
Tariki, 15
Tatari, 49
Tatemae, 116
Tea ceremony, 10, 21, 105
Team work, 19
Tendai sect, 12, 14
Terakoya, 56
TESOL (Teaching English Abroad), 62
Three Character Classics, 56
Three Treasures, 22, 34, 35
Tohoku disaster (2011), 49–50, 57
Tokugawa period
  Buddhism, 31
  education, 55–56, 58
Tradition, 71
Transmigration, 22, 23, 24, 34

Uji (clan), 11, 42
U.S. Occupation, 38, 54, 56

Warrior culture, 14, 15
Westminster Confession of Faith, 86, 89–90
Westminster Shorter Catechism, 53, 91
World War II, 37, 56

Youth culture, 77

Zazen, 16, 19, 23
Zen, 10, 13, 15–17, 19, 66f

Scripture Index

Genesis
1	1, 23–24
17	7, 66
32	28, 51

Exodus
20	2–6, 47

Deuteronomy
11	18–19, 59

Numbers
4	3, 71

Joshua
6	2–5, 117

Psalms
16	11, 92
19	1–2, 12–14, 92
26	3, 119
89	15, 119

Proverbs
22	6, 59

Ecclesiastes
7	1, 33

Isaiah
6	3, 92
54	2, 93

Joel
1	3, 60

Matthew
6	6, 71
11	11, 28, 52, 113, 119
13	18–23, 117
25	24–25, 102
26	2, 31–33
28	19, 112

Mark
15	18, 101

Luke
2	46–47, 71
9	23, 62
14	26, 66
15	13, 67
23	39–43, 20
24	13–16, 84

John
13	14, 2
17	3, 25
19	30, 91

Acts
8	24–40, 72

Scripture Index

Acts *(continued)*
17	22–25, 49
20	9, 102

Romans
1	16–17, 87
3	21–24, 88, 89
5	12–21, 91
9	19–20, 19, 51

I Corinthians
7	14, 28
8	41
13	4, 28
15	12–14, 33, 34, 55

II Corinthians
5	21, 90

Galatians
3	29, 66

Ephesians
2	1–4, 88
2	5–9, 88–89

Philippians
1	21–23, 33, 79
4	4–7, 23

Colossians
1	13–14, 90
4	12–13, 15, 102, 106

II Timothy
3	1–4, 8–12, 79, 97

Hebrews
4	12, 119
9	27, 24
12	6, 78

II Peter
1	3, 21, 85, 86

www.ingramcontent.com/pod-product-compliance
Lightning Source LLC
Chambersburg PA
CBHW071623170426
43195CB00038B/2043